The Islands of The

CARIBBEAN SEA

A Colorful and Concise History

To
Johnny, Ronnie, Nick and William

Copyright 1992 JSA Publications, Inc.

Scrivener Press
P.O. Box 37175
Oak Park, MI 48237

First Edition 1992
ISBN: 0-929957-02-4
Library of Congress Catalog Number 91-62783
Printed in the United States of America
2 3 4 5 6 7 8 9 0

Additional copies of this and our other books maybe ordered by calling 1-800-345-0096

Carrib.   ISBN   0-929957-02-4

The Islands of The

A Colorful and Concise History

by

Joe Ajlouny

Scrivener Press

ACKNOWLEDGEMENTS

Thanks are due to the following for their help, support and encouragement:

June I. Parker, Lisa A. McDonald, Marilyn Krol, Terri Rogers, Susan Graham, Christian Klaver, Janet Puttick, Mike Easthope. Each of them owns a part of my heart and I am grateful for all their assistance.

My sincere thanks to Felix Mattei, Meredith Head, Tony Bridge and Reinier Heere for their valiant efforts. Thanks also to Jerrold Jenkins, Tim Shaub and their staff at Publishers Distribution Service. Lastly, extra special thanks to my parents, family and friends for their support and encouragement. It means the world to me.

Graphic design by June I. Parker and Joanne Nicola. Maps courtesy of U.S. State Department Office of Public Affairs. Cover Photography by T.Grief, Inter Design Ltd.

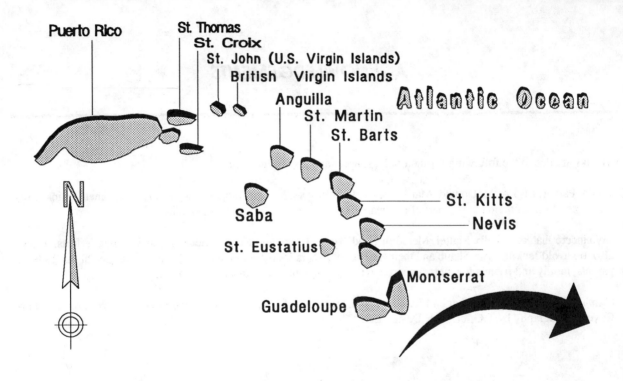

INTRODUCTION

The islands of the Caribbean Sea sprawl over a vast area of the tropics zone between the continents of North and South America. Though numbering in the hundreds, most of the islands are small and uninhabited except by the birds above and the fish below. Of those that are populated, tremendous differences resulted from their varying historical, colonial, social and economic experiences. As we shall see, geography played a large part in the story as well. This book seeks to help one understand how these differences arose and the consequences that they have had for the peoples of each island community. As such, this brief historical account is ideal for tourists who wish to familiarize themselves with the people and places they so eagerly visit. In this day and age, more tourists, mostly from the United States and Canada, but increasingly from Europe and Latin America, will vacation on the islands of the Caribbean Sea than anywhere else in the world.

Whereas the numerous islands of the Caribbean are necessarily different for the reasons stated above, they just as necessarily share many common qualities and characteristics. Thus, there is a certain similarity about the islands, but as you will learn, this cannot be stretched into a general "uniformity." Many accounts by early European adventurers have aptly described the islands as "sisters." This seems to me to be the best explanation of their individuality, for just as sisters are born of the same blood, each nonetheless develops individually and grows to become unique unto herself. The majority of the islands of the Caribbean Sea were discovered by the great sailor Christopher Columbus on his four voyages to the New World between the years 1492 to 1504. Most of us know that Columbus sailed in search of a westward passage to the Orient. Once there, he hoped to win commercial concessions for the Spanish monarchy. But Columbus and all of the other cartographers of the day were woefully wrong about the actual size of the earth. Instead of discovering India, Columbus and his crew stumbled into the Americas. He named the islands the West Indies and the sea the Caribbean, after the native Carib Indians. Both names stuck. Accordingly, Columbus claimed each island in the name of the recently unified Spanish throne and renamed most of them to suit his fancies.

Yet it is, of course, erroneous to say that Columbus actually "discovered" the many islands upon whose shores he happened to float. In reality, the majority of the islands were inhabited by communities of native Americans who were no doubt startled to find Columbus' big ships resting in their quiet bays. These peoples had their own languages and cultures and a heritage that dates back at least as long ago as Europe's. As you shall learn, the landing of the white man had disastrous conse-quences for these simple peoples, despite the ostensible claims of the Europeans that they had come to "civilize and baptize" them pursuant to Christian customs.

Following Spain to the region were Portugal, Britain, France, the Netherlands and others. These great powers of the age were likewise in search of new trading routes, and the wealth and prestige that accompanied them. So rapid was the conquest of the entire area that by 1675, all of the islands had been claimed, if not colonized, by Europe's great monarchies. Competition for land, resources and especially gold caused much friction and frequent wars between them. The entire region was patrolled by marauding groups of wayward and desperate sailors. From these groups the pirates and buccaneers of old arose, and with them, much of the legend and folklore of the Caribbean Sea did too. For centuries the islands lingered on their own or at the bidding of sea lords and colonial governors. The scourge of slavery destroyed the native population and severely impacted those who were imported to replace them. It may have been paradise but life was anything but easy.

In the 20th century, the colonial rule of Europe's great powers, hastened by two world wars, began to break down. Many of the islands declared political independence. Others obtained self rule, while at the same time choosing to maintain their ties as territories or possessions of their mother governments. The cycle of travail and poverty, which all of the islands experienced to one degree or another, was lessened in part by the growth of commercial trade links and with the rise of tourism as an industry. In recent years, offshore oil drilling, light manufacturing and international finance have found a home under the Caribbean sun.

Today the permanent inhabitants of the islands, most of whom are the descendants of African slaves, are still engaged in a struggle for economic and social advancement. Their cultures and contributions are commonplace throughout North America, from food to music, to fashion and literature. This being the case, a proper understanding of the history of these peoples and their island homes is necessary before one can truly appreciate the beauty and diversity of the islands and the peoples themselves. I admonish you to ask questions and be otherwise curious as you travel around. You will be fascinated by what you will learn.

J.A.

CONTENTS

ost historical accounts of the region now commonly called the Caribbean Basin begin with a singular event: the arrival of Columbus. As the introductory remarks explained, this is not at all accurate, or for that matter fair.* Long before the Europeans landed in the "New World" it was sparsely populated by natives of a thousand or more tribes. So great was the bounty of the land and sea that they generally lived peacefully and independently of each other. Commerce between tribes was scarce and none are believed to have developed a written language. One can only argue that Spain's conquest and settlement began the "recorded history" of the region.

The fact that the islands of the Caribbean Sea are still called the "West Indies" is proof of the enduring influence of that initial voyage.

Due to the vastness of the area, it is necessary to first describe it in terms of its geographic position in relation to the two continental mainlands it rests between. To do this, one must first adopt the common nomenclature as devised by the Europeans a long time ago.

The great sprawling arc of island masses that make up the West Indies is conveniently comprised of two major groups: the Greater Antilles and the Lesser Antilles. The first group includes the large islands of Cuba, Hispaniola, (Haiti and Dominican Republic), Jamaica and Puerto Rico. The latter consists of a multitude of mismatched islands which swing southeasterly toward the Venezuelan coastline. Within the Lesser Antilles lay the two archipelago chains known as the Leeward Islands and the Windward Islands, which trail off to the south, ending abruptly with Grenada. Trinidad and Tobago are situated one hundred miles south but are not considered part of either grouping.

The entire area exists as the result of a submerged continental tract which geologists now believe once connected North and South America. The islands themselves, with some exceptions, but especially those of the Greater Antilles, are really just the tops of submerged mountain ranges. They have left lofty cliffs and limestone formations on Jamaica and Hispaniola and to a lesser extent on Cuba, Puerto Rico, Dominica and Martinique. Several of the islands emerged as a result of underwater volcanoes and still others were created out of wreckages of rock and coral reefs which collected sand and silt through the ages.

As always, the unyielding effects of erosion, subterranean activity, storms and tides wrought on each island a degree of uniqueness that only mother nature and time can produce. Natural harbors, inland lakes, mangrove swamps, peninsulas of all shapes and diverse terrains were formed throughout the region, but to differing degrees depending on the specific geological condi-

tions. Among the other characteristics found on the islands are waterfalls, hot springs, rivers and creeks, forests, rocky hills, limestone and ignatius plains, dry and fragmented slopes, craters, and on Guadeloupe and Martinique, non-dormant volcanos. The quality of the topsoil ranges from very fertile to arid and scrubby. Vegetation and fauna grew prolifically while birds, reptiles and rodent populations remained static. The climate, being tropical, never varied significantly from warm and balmy to hot and humid.

Unto these small islands ventured the aboriginal natives of South and Central America. Though dates are uncertain, it is estimated that the first islands were gradually inhabited during the 4th through 10th centuries. We know today that Indian civilizations were highly developed during that period throughout the Western Hemisphere. It is suggested that the natives of South America first migrated northeasterly through Venezuela's Orinco river valley in search of tropical weather and bountiful fishing grounds. Warfare between differing tribes no doubt also played a role in the migratory phase, as did drought, ritual and wanderlust.

The natives that finally settled the islands have become known as the Arawaks. They were a simple and peaceful people who lived in small seaside communities of thatched huts. For the most part they lived off the sea, but supplemented their diets by hunting small game and growing crops of maize, beans and cassava root. They also cultivated a potent ceremonial,smoking herb, they called *cohiba* which was used for recreational, medicinal and ritualistic purposes.* The hierarchy of a typical Arawak village was presided over by a local chief, called a Cacique, who was typically an elder from a prominent clan. Beneath him came the clan leaders, native warriors and lowly native peasants. Men fished and hunted while women tended to the villages and crops and raised the children. The spiritual practices of the Arawaks are not well understood and have only been surmised after

---

The pipe used to smoke the cohiba was called a tobak. The Spaniards, who were much delighted with this custom, sent samples back to Europe, but oddly enough called the leaves "tobacco" instead of the pipe!

It has been widely speculated that local legend predicted the coming of earthly-gods and that the arrival of Columbus was a fulfillment of the prophecy. The extent to which the natives believed the Europeans were gods is probably overstated.

careful excavation of village remains and burial grounds. They no doubt ascribed to a myriad of gods the unexplainable questions of their time. Among the artifacts uncovered from their civilization are carved wood deities, clay pots, stone tools, woven baskets and mats, small pieces of furniture and decorative accessories. The Arawaks apparently never discovered the wheel or learned to domesticate animals. They traveled to fishing waters in hollowed out tree trunks. They had no knowledge of money, precious metals or stones and most importantly, no alphabet or system of writing.

The accounts of the Spaniards describe the appearance and behavior of the Arawaks and their cousins, the Lucayans of the Bahamas, the Ciboney of Cuba, the Tainos of Hispaniola and the Caribs of the southern islands. The men were short and dark and their bodies were painted with wild colors and designs. They had straight black hair which they wore short in front and long in back. The women were described as dark and rugged with long hair and large breasts. Communal social order was rigid and ceremonial festivities were the highlight of each new season.

The natives covered themselves with body colors and ornaments of shells, bones, shark teeth, feathers and beads. Some wore gold plugs in their noses and ears. The heads of male babies were pressed flat in the rear by pressure applied from wooden boards. As a sign of maturity, some Arawak boys had their right ears chopped off. The average girl gave birth by age fifteen. Then Columbus arrived.

Columbus first landed on the Bahaman island of Guanahani (now called San Salvador) on October 12, 1492. The natives would withdrew into the woods to await a sign. When several small boats made their way to shore, the natives slowly lost their skepticism and within the day were heartily welcoming their visitors. One can also imagine the feelings of the sailors who, after nearly staging a mutiny against Columbus, rejoiced in his name. There, around them in boats, were curious brown men and women waving and smiling. What a sight it must have been; their sense of excitement and relief must have been great indeed.

To the innocent native islanders, the arrival of the white man was an unbelievable occurrence. Whereas the Europeans, by 1492 had experience with native peoples in Africa, the Azores and Canary Islands, the Arawaks had no expectation of nor knowledge of any other civilization beyond their own. They had only marginal contacts with neighboring tribes, obviously finding isolation preferable to warfare. With the absence of enmity, they grew docile and friendly. Thus, Columbus' dispatches to Queen Isabela described the natives as wild, but "a people who would become good servants." Their eagerness to please, and their trade with the Spaniards for the bizarre items they had brought, like cattle and sheep -- and nails and buckets -- can scarcely be imagined. By the use of sign language, rudimentary communication was possible. Columbus immediately noticed the bits of gold they wore and inquired as to its origin.

That simple question changed the world, for as we shall see, the Spaniards had a definite mission in mind: the search for wealth, spices and new trading routes. For the Lucayans and subsequently all the Arawak peoples, the arrival of Columbus was the beginning of the end. Little did they know that their visitors would use and enslave them, steal their land and drive them into virtual extinction. Remember, this was all done pursuant to "holy" endeavors. Let's now travel across the Atlantic and assess the scene in Europe at that time.

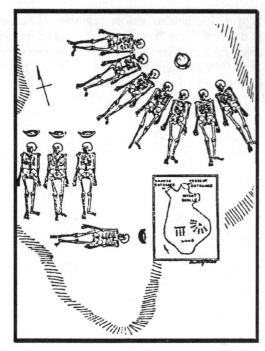

An Arawak tomb as discovered in a cave. The significance of the arrangement of the corpses has not been determined.

hen we were children we learned that people used to think the earth was flat and that it was Columbus that proved them wrong. Actually, by the middle of the 15th century, it was well accepted that the earth was indeed round and that it could therefore be circum-navigated. This spawned the shipbuilding industry to develop new and larger boats to meet this challenge. In the 1450's the Portuguese were the undisputed leaders in Europe in the art of maritime exploration. They were the first to explore the west African coastline, after first exploring the Azores and Madeira islands in the northern Atlantic Ocean.

Naturally, these early successes only stiffened European rivalry and competition for wealth and conquest. The goods the Portuguese brought back from Africa, gems, ivory and silver, gave new meaning to the tales of

Marco Polo's exciting travels two centuries before. It was Polo, who in 1275, had reached an overland route to the eastern civilizations of the Orient. The riches and goods discovered there, such as tea and spices, utterly changed European life. The most significant find of that era from the east was, of course, gunpowder. But the eastern caravan route was problematic. It took Polo and his entourage five years to reach ancient China, which he called Cathay. With the rise of the Ottoman empire in the Middle East, the land route was discourteously closed.

The Turks, however, had their price for permitting trade with the Khans of the Orient. The merchant lords of Italy, particularly Florence, Venice, Naples and Genoa, were only too eager to pay it. With the increase in trade came a demand for new and larger ships, experienced sailors, port facilities, financial and legal insti-

A scroll depicting brothers Marco and Niccolo Polo with their caravan.

tutions and for enterprises to support them. Trade and money increasingly became the means of exchange, replacing the barter of goods and pledging of assets as the basis for commercial relations.

For the "old world" it was a time of great change, a period called the Renaissance, from the French word for "rebirth." New ideas and forgotten ones were being discussed and exchanged like never before. The Catholic Church still played a highly influential role on the continent and frequently lashed out at "heretical teachings" which it feared could undermine its power. In Spain, the repressive Inquisition dealt harshly with anything remotely suggesting change in the established world view. But tears in the old seam were inevitable. The next half century witnessed great social change, most importantly a split in the church, the Reformation and a relaxation of numerous prohibitions and restrictions.

The 15th century was also the cradle of modern scientific observation and experimentation. In this period the true characteristics of earth and nature were

Christopher Columbus
(1451-1526)
The famous navigator is known as Christoforo Columbo in Italy and as Cristóbal Colón in Spain

being discovered, and in some cases rediscovered. The names of Galileo, Copernicus, Toscanelli and other discoverers owe their historical legacy to this era. Alongside the scientific inquiry came a blossoming of art and music, and court life in the great mansions of the aristocrats. The European artistic and architectural magnificence of the era have never been equaled by any people. It was, in short, the dawn of a new age, the Age of Enlightenment.

To this time came the opportunities of naval exploration and trade links with new peoples. Each noble house saw in the seas a mechanism for prestige and prosperity. One by one, the monarchies of Europe commissioned naval expeditions in all directions. They charged their subjects to explore, and if need be, conquer. Nothing would stand in the way of their success.

With improvements in the size and strength of ships and in navigational instruments, commerce was bound to explode. By 1475, sea routes were established to Constantinople, the Crimea, Smyrna, Carthage and elsewhere. Competition between nations often caused distrust and friction, which frequently erupted into warfare.

The competition extended beyond territorial claims to the allegiance of experienced sea captains. One such man was a Genoese-born sailor named Christopher Columbus.

Columbus had joined a galley crew at age 14 and survived a sea battle that brought him alone on a floating wooden plank to Portugal. There he married, worked for his brother-in-law as a merchant and began studying shipping routes. Columbus then conceived a design for a passage to India and China by sailing westward, as the eastern route was owned by the Portuguese and backed by a Papal decree.

The eager Columbus applied for sponsorship of his planned expedition to John II of Portugal and Henry VII of England. They both rejected the proposal as too risky. Isabella, Queen of Castille (John II's daughter), who in 1469 married Ferdinand V of Aragon, was not discouraged by the seeming implausibility of the plan. Rather than rejecting him outright, she referred the matter to a panel of advisors. After almost eight years of on again - off again discussions, Columbus finally received approval in January, 1492.

On Friday, August 3rd, Columbus set sail aboard the carrack *Santa Maria* with 50 men, attended by two smaller caravel ship the *Pinta* and the *Nina*, with crews of about 30 men each. After a brief stop in the Canary Islands, they set out on what has become the single most important voyage in history.

Columbus' diary describes the difficulties he encountered with the sea, navigation and most importantly, his impatient crew. They had been out to sea longer than any known voyage to that time. Then, in the second week of October, branches were spotted in the water, which was turning from dark blue to turquoise green. On October 12th, one Rodrigo de Triana looked out on the Pinta's forecastle, shouted excitedly "Tierra, Tierra!" . It was land at last. It being too dangerous to proceed with darkness nearing, Columbus ordered the sails taken down for fear of grounding or encountering reefs. That night, nobody slept.

What the voyagers didn't know was that they had landed on the island of *Guanahani*, a small low rock formation that stands on the outside edge of the North American continental plate. The island was sparsely occupied by a tribe of Arawaks, the Lucayans. These peaceful people had come to this and countless surrounding isles in flight from the cannibalistic Carib tribe of the South American mainland.

As described earlier, contacts between the two peoples were quickly established. Columbus reported: "The banks of rivers are embedded with lofty palm trees, whose shade gives a delicious freshness to the air, and the birds and the flowers are uncommon and bountiful. I was so delighted with the scene, that I had almost come to the resolution of staying here for the remainder of my days; for believe me, sire, these countries far surpass all the rest of the world in beauty and convenience."

When Columbus asked the natives where he could find gold, they spoke of the land to the south they called Cubla (Cuba). Columbus thought that they must have been referring to Kublai, as in the Khan of China. After only two days, the anxious Spaniards set out once again in search of riches. Unbeknownst to the Lucayans, however, they first planted their flag and renamed the island San Salvador, in honor of the Savior.

For the following 20 days, Columbus hopped from one island to another, renaming them all and likewise claiming them for Spain's dominion. He brought about a half dozen Lucayans with him to help navigate the shallow, but treacherous sea lanes. Columbus called the area *bajamar*, meaning "shallow sea." It is from this observation, noted in his diary, that the islands came to be called the Bahamas. The islands of the Caribbean were literally next door.

olumbus and his crew sailed on from the Bahamas to the east coast of Cuba, which he renamed Juana. After a few days of scouting, they sailed east to the island of *Basio*, which Columbus renamed Hispaniola, meaning "Little Spain." In both places they met and bartered with the natives, without serious incident or mishap. The Spaniards decided that their fortunes would best be served by the establishment of a settlement on Hispaniola's northeast shore. Thus, La Navidad, a small fort overlooking the sea became the first European settlement in the New World. On January 16, 1493 Columbus and his crew, with only two ships left, set their sails for home. They left 39 men and all the provisions they could spare at the fort. They began the rise of New Spain. The vast conquests she would reap in the Western Hemisphere took the name the Spanish Main.

Whereas Columbus had not really "discovered" the New World, he was certainly responsible for "linking" it to Europe. Upon his return to Spain, he had no trouble convincing the government that he had made a truly fantastic discovery. Preparations were immediately started for his return trip, this time with large boats and crews, and provisions enough for a long and prosperous voyage. Columbus' return to Spain was a great event and large scale celebrations were thrown in his honor. All along Columbus knew that he had to justify the expense of his first mission. The "cups of gold" he brought with him, as well as several Arawak natives he kidnapped, were all the justification he needed. Word of his discovery traveled very quickly. Spain issued edicts declaring the route to the New World was hers and hers alone, and successfully enlisted the Pope in support of her claims. In return, the Catholic Church was promised a share of the spoils and the right to send Jesuit missionaries on all of Spain's subsequent voyages.

The second expedition to the New World began in September, 1493. Led again by Columbus, who was now an admiral (in addition to his title of Royal Governor), the force comprised seventeen different ships with a total passenger count of 1,200. Among those on board were sailors, artists, scientists, Jesuits, settler/farmers and enough livestock to begin several ranches on Hispaniola. Two ships were filled with agricultural stock such as fruit trees, plants and seeds; two others were packed with construction supplies. They carried no heavy weapons and no commercial cargo, except what they expected to barter to the natives. The sole object of the expedition was to establish a single permanent settlement on Hispaniola from which mining and farming could be commenced.

This time Columbus took a more southerly route and bypassed the Bahamas altogether. He sailed to and

Spain stakes its claim to the New World.

charted the small islands that make up the Lesser Antilles, including Dominica, Guadeloupe, Nevis and Santa Cruz. They proceeded northward and discovered the Virgin Islands and Puerto Rico. He then sailed westward to La Navidad to rescue his mates who had stayed behind. But when he arrived, he was surprised to see it completely abandoned.

The expedition quickly disembarked and established a new settlement nearby called Isabela, in honor of his queen. The Spaniards enlisted the help of the native people, the Tainos, to construct a fort and town. In return, Columbus promised to protect and defend them from enemies and baptize them to the Christian faith. This system of managing the natives was called *repartimiento*; it was but an excuse to enslave the natives to work as miners, farm laborers or servants. Of the original 39 Europeans who stayed at La Navidad, only a handful were ever found, the rest having perished or gone into the woods never to be heard from again. Within two months, the settlers had made great progress. They cleared land, erected buildings and a church and began the exploration of the island's interior in search of gold and silver mines.

But problems soon developed. First, disagreements erupted between the settlers and soon entangled Columbus and his lieutenants in endless squabbles. Next, the Tainos came to reject their subjugation and many fled the farms and mines to which they were assigned to work. As if to get away from this state of affairs, Columbus set off with three ships to do more exploring in the summer of 1495.

They traveled westward around the horn of Hispaniola and along the south coast of Cuba. They then headed south and discovered Jamaica, which was called *Xaymaca*, "land of wood and water" by the local Arawaks. Upon his return he found matters at Isabela had degenerated significantly. Not only were the settlers at each other's throats, but most were ill and restless. What's more, the Tainos were now in open revolt and had stolen goods of all kinds from the guarded storehouses of the settlement. The exasperated admiral decided to return to Spain to enlist more aid and settlers, but most importantly to obtain instructions from the government on how to deal with the trouble which he had encountered. Before he left in the spring of 1496, a new expedition from Spain had reached Isabela which fortunately brought badly needed supplies and medicine to the distraught settlers. The arrival was heartening and convinced them that they had not been forgotten, as they had feared.

In his absence, Columbus' brother Bartolome was placed in charge. Within a short time, it was decided to evacuate the settlement in favor of a spot on the southern coastal region which they called Santo Domingo. This city, which still thrives today as the capital city of the nation in the Dominican Republic, was to become the headquarters of the Spanish Main for the next 50 years. Again, land was cleared and a new town was built. Bartolome issued land grants and titles to rebels in order to avoid mischief. He awarded recaptured Tainos islanders to estate owners as slave labor. He also ordered the majority of the natives into the mines and imposed a gold dust tax far in excess of their ability to deliver.

Columbus arrived for a third time in 1498. He reached Santo Domingo after having first discovered the islands of Trinidad and Tobago, and Venezuela on the mainland of South America. He found a group of settlers in rebellion against the authority of Bartolome. By this time complaints about the Santo Domingo settlement had reached Spain and the government appointed a new governor to supersede Columbus' authority. Francisco de Bobadilla arrived in 1499 and in no time at all restored order by brute force. He had Columbus arrested and ordered him returned to Spain in leg irons. His successor Nicolas de Ovando was perhaps the governor most responsible for Spain's early conquest of the New World. It was Ovando who created the new economic system called the *Ecomienda,* which called for the impressing of all natives as plantation workers and all settlers as subject to the orders of naval commanders. Today, we might call such measures a declaration of "martial law."

From 1500 onward, Spain sent numerous voyagers to the New World. New settlements were started on Cuba,

Jamaica and Puerto Rico and volunteers were enlisted to try their fortunes under the warm sun on the other side of the world. The toll that this expansion took on the native islanders was in all cases, very costly. Not only were they worked to death, but they had become infected with diseases such as smallpox, typhoid and gonorrhea diseases which their virgin bodies could not bear.. Those that did not succumb to cruelty or scourge, committed suicide or ran off in to the interior never to be seen again. It was clear that the Europeans who came to "save them" were the cause of their doom. Despite the efforts of many courageous missionaries, the natives were wiped out as a race. On Hispaniola, for example, the Tainos were basically extinct by 1560.

Life on the islands was hardly paradise for the Spaniards either. The stark conditions they found themselves in convinced many that their expectations had been too great. While there were certainly many accomplishments for which, to the European mind, they could be proud, the future remained uncertain. By the 1520's, Spain had turned her sights to Mexico and Peru in an attempt to recover her huge investment in men and money. As we now know, these moves gained her much wealth. Sadly, Spain's gains were the Arawaks', the Mayas', the Aztecs' and the Incas' loss.

Before we turn to the stories of the founding of the "modern history" of the islands, a last word about Christopher Columbus is in order. After his humiliating defeat by Bobadilla, Columbus was restored to his titles in Spain and made one last voyage to the New World in 1502. Until his death, he always believed he had found the eastern islands of Asia. It was not until the voyages of Balboa of Spain and Magellan of Portugal that the Pacific Ocean was discovered and crossed. It was only then that the true size of the earth was fully realized.

Scholars have surmised that Columbus had been convinced of his error during his lifetime because the area's islands were called the *Antillas* (Antilles) which is Spanish for "Atlantis." At a time when fanciful stories were frequently regarded as true, it is not difficult to see how many Europeans believed the islands of the Caribbean Sea were the remnants of the legendary lost continent.

It was, after all, at this time, that Spanish naval captain Juan Ponce de Leon claimed he discovered the Fountain of Youth in the Bahamas.

Columbus retired after his final return in 1503. His fourth voyage had been filled with tribulation and difficulty. No doubt he felt betrayed; the victim of jealousy for his successes and discrimination due to his birth in Italy and upbringing in Portugal, Spain's ever present enemies. He died in Spain in 1506 and was buried in a monastery near Seville. In 1536 his remains and those of his son and companion were transferred to Santo Domingo. In 1796, they were transferred again, this time, to a cathedral in Havana. Then in 1899, upon Spain's final defeat in the Spanish-American War, they were sent home to Spain where they remain in the beautiful Renaissance cathedral of Seville. Bartolome Columbus died in Cuba in 1514.

s already noted, the Spaniards established the first settlement in the New World on the large and mountainous island of Hispaniola. The reason for their choice was clear: their expectation of finding gold and other precious metals. The fort at La Navidad, which means "the birth" in Spanish, was however, a sorry way to start. The 39 sailors left there by Columbus in 1493 were completely unequipped to handle their isolation. Had it not been for the destruction of the flagship *Santa Maria* in a storm off her eastern coast, it is unlikely that a settlement would have ever been attempted there.

But history is as much the study of accidental events as it is those that were deliberate. The abandonment of La Navidad by 1494 led to the establishment of Isabela in the nearby hills overlooking the natural harbor Samana. The Spaniards enticed the allegiance of the native Tainos by exchanging goods and gifts with them. The Tainos were employed as scouts and showed the settlers where they could obtain fresh water from mountain springs, and caves where they could seek shelter from frequent storms. But for a variety of reasons, Isabela did not prosper. The soil proved too weak to support the crops that had been planted. The windy hills and dangerous reptiles also encouraged the settlers to move to the southern coastal plain where they founded Santo Domingo in 1496. It was at Santo Domingo that lessons were learned and new methods of farming and administration were introduced. These changes, as well as the arrival of new Spanish leadership who were trained to manage such ventures, ensured that New Spain would not wither away, but would prosper and grow larger than anyone could have ever imagined.

The island of Hispaniola is 30,000 square miles in

An early astronomer taking navigational measurements. It was inventions such as this compass that made ocean exploration possible.

size and after Cuba, is the second largest island of the Caribbean Sea. Its humble beginnings were greatly exceeded by virtue of being chosen the capital of the Spanish Main. Despite being situated in the heart of the Caribbean, her central mountainous region is subject to significant climatic variations. The cooler temperature and greater rainfall in the interior valleys and peaks is further influenced by the strong northeast trade winds that wail across the Sea. Hispaniola is home to the highest peak in the region, Pico Duarte, which rises to the height of 10,400 feet above the sea.

The troubles that the early settlers encountered with the natives have been described. The consequences these troubles produced significantly injured the purpose of the settlement itself. For within a very short time, an acute labor shortage developed. This shortage was the result of two simple processes: the destruction of the Tainos and the deaths of able-bodied settlers. The problem was further aggravated by the rush to establish other settlements both on Hispaniola and other islands. Try as she did to send more men and ships, Spain struggled to satisfy the needs of her new frontier.

The surviving accounts of many writers relate stories of incredible sadness, neglect and cruelty. Not only were the natives hurting, but so too were the settlers and their families. The hardships of disease, droughts and storms all combined to create a disposition on the island far less sunny than one might otherwise expect. Due to the shortage of manpower, Governor Ovando obtained permission to capture the Lucayans of the Bahama islands and distributed them to work where they were most needed. Accordingly, they were effectively enslaved throughout the estates and quarries of Hispaniola and Cuba. By 1580, the Lucayans were wiped out just as the Tainos had been before them.

As wanderlust, curiosity - and the thirst for gold - increased, large segments of Hispaniola's population resettled elsewhere, principally in Cuba. The fertile soil and extensive gold deposits quickly made Cuba's main settlement of Santiago a desirable place to settle in. Ovando's second-in-command, Diego Velazquez, himself a disciplinarian and administrator of considerable authority, led the conquest of Cuba in 1511. Within five years, seven different settlements had been established along her southern shores. It was Velazquez who sent the most infamous of all the conquistadors, Hernando Cortez, to conquer Mexico.

From Hispaniola, the Spaniards settled Puerto Rico and, to a lesser extent, Jamaica. They also sailed south to Venezuela and settled both Trinidad and Tobago at the mouth of the Orinico river valley. It was via this river that the Spaniards first delved into the interiors of the South American mainland. Each new expedition that sailed from Santo Domingo weakened her in terms of men and supplies. Though it would remain the capital of New Spain, its importance as a settlement shifted from a main population center to the main launch for other islands. As such, Santo Domingo became the operations and logistical headquarters for New Spain. While the adventurers sailed away, the stability of the town strengthened and its economy slowly began to improve. Henceforth, Santo Domingo's farms and markets served the needs of the new commercial traffic in

the sea. No ships returned to Spain with booty without first stopping there for provisions, and to carry messages and reports back to the Spanish government.

Back home in Spain, King Ferdinand had died and Queen Isabella gradually grew insane. They were succeeded to the throne by their grandson Charles V, Spain's greatest king. Though he was only 21 years old, Charles was very keen on New Spain's potential. He encouraged more people to settle in the New World and for the first time invited Portuguese, German and Dutch citizens to settle in return for Spanish protection. This

Charles V
(1500-1558)

Though he is known as Charles I of Spain, he was also Charles V, Holy Roman Emperor. His vast conquests against his European neighbors, principally France and Italy, but also upon Germany and England, earned him numerous other titles.

was a brilliant move because it brought builders, craftsmen, and artisans to Santo Domingo and elsewhere, where they were badly needed. But as history has shown, Charles was more interested in the conquest of Europe, particularly of France and Italian principalities at war with his ally, Naples. He saw the islands only as a means of bolstering his reputation in Europe. This prejudice resulted in a policy of exploitation instead of development. This was a legacy that would often be repeated.

In succeeding years, the role of Santo Domingo was eclipsed by the rise in importance of the Cuban settlement of Havana. By the year 1600, Havana, Cartagena and Mexico City became regional headquarters in the Spanish colonization of the Americas. Ranching of cattle, with its production of meat and hides, became Hispaniola's lasting contribution to Spain's efforts. Alongside cattle ranches, large farming estates were either granted to or purchased by Europeans who promised to stay and live on the island. Very soon grapes, olives, lemons, rice, wheat, tomatoes and many other products were raised on Hispaniola's plantations. Some of these crops eventually failed, but it did not prevent others from trying their luck in the fields. As always, labor was in great demand. This was a feature of the economy until Black Africans were imported to supplement the precious few natives left*

The enmity which the great European powers shared at home inevitably followed them to the New World. Thus, the English, French, Portuguese and later the Dutch, being jealous of Spain's discoveries, quickly decided to "join the party". The sudden arrival of these powers changed the New World. Unfortunately for Spain, this was usually at her expense. The English and French knew the New World was simply too large an area for Spain to conquer by herself. So they decided there was plenty of room for them to conquer too. Portugal, on the other hand, had a treaty with Spain which ceded shipping routes in its favor. For this reason, Portugal began the colonization of Brazil, not wishing

---

Like most governments of the day, Spain was not above the employment of convict labor on particularly difficult and dangerous undertakings.

to "bother" with the comparatively small and poor islands of the Caribbean. This left the Dutch in a different situation. Their great contribution to naval expeditionary history was the settlement of the East Indies, principally, present day Indonesia in the 15th century. For fear of being left out, they too made claim to possessions in the West Indies.

The importance of Spanish shipping and her lack of defense, encouraged these powers to privately support attacks against Spain in the New World. Thus began the story of the "privateers," bands of floating mercenaries who were hired to act as surrogate navies. It was from these privateers that the legend and legacy of the pirates and buccaneers of the Caribbean Sea came to be told. The losses these forces inflicted on Spanish commerce were staggering. In the mid-1530's, France in particular used privateers to attack Spain in the Bahamas and Puerto Rico. For example, Hispaniola's second largest settlement of Yaguana was attacked and occupied by the French in 1537. France adopted this policy in retaliation for Charles V's defeat of them throughout Europe. The British, who were eager to cash in on Spain's new found wealth, did not hesitate to employ similar means. History reveals that many of the new generations of naval explorers whose services they retained, first acquired their experience as privateers in the Caribbean Sea.

In 1553, a French armada under the command of Francois Le Clerk began a program of pillaging and burning lightly protected Spanish settlements throughout the West Indies. After capturing Santiago, they attacked Havana. Remarkably, they took control of the town without a battle. The governor and all the people had retreated to the interior with everything they could carry. The French demanded a ransom before they would leave. It was not paid, so in 1555 they burned Havana to the ground. These episodes, tragic as they are, were but the beginning of about 200 years of continual hit and run raiding and plundering by all the colonizers of the region against each other. Though peace treaties were regularly signed, they were usually either ignored or eventually repudiated. The huge potential which all the great powers saw in the Americas was just too great a temptation to behave peaceably.

Then in 1585, the great English navigator Frances Drake began fleet operations in the West Indies. He was no stranger to the area, having spent almost 15 years in and out of Caribbean waters under the command of privateer John Hawkins. His circumnavigation of the world during the years 1577-1580 made him a genuine naval hero. Drake's plan was to make a bold, multi-pronged attack on Spanish possessions throughout the region. He sailed with 20 ships and more than 1,600 men. Like the French before him, the purpose of his mission was to permanently dislodge Spain's defenses, which had been substantially improved in the ensuing 30 years. Unlike the French, however, Drake cleverly rounded up bands of runaway Indians called "Maroons" to help him and his men. As one can imagine, it probably wasn't difficult to convince the surviving natives to attack New Spain. The usual plan of operation provided for a frontal attack by the British seamen in conjunction with a rear attack by the natives from the interior.

Drake's first target was Santo Domingo, the capital of New Spain. With the advantage of surprise, he captured the city and held it ransom for about a month. Upon payment to his satisfaction, the British withdrew, looting and destroying everything in their path. Santo Domingo was a ruined city and unfortunately, never regained her prominence again. Next, the English set their sights on Cartagena, the important Spanish settlement on the Venezuelan coast. Drake knew that Spain used Cartagena as a main depot for their gold prior to shipping it home.

The attack proved far more difficult and costly for Drake and his men. By the time they scaled the coast and plowed through to the center of town, the Spaniards had withdrawn to the hills with everything of value. For the following six weeks, while negotiations for ransom were being conducted, Drake's company was hit by an epidemic which caused great losses of men and horses. When they finally capitulated, they were weak and demoralized. They escaped to the Cayman Islands and thereafter returned home with ample gold and stories to tell.

Thus, by the dawn of the 17th century, Spain's possessions in the New World, though injured, remained intact. The settlers who survived were used to hardship so in no time they rebuilt razed towns. Most importantly, Spain's supply system and lines of communications remained essentially undisturbed. The reason for the failure by both the French and British attackers was the simple fact that the entire area was just too vast and the distance too far to maintain continued pressure. Spain's head start had given her a great advantage in terms of wealth and control of strategic points. Moreover, the heat, famine, disease and other hardships that seagoing ventures experienced at that time served to favor the defenders. Spain's first 100 years of occupation in America were on the whole, very successful. In Europe, however, the once mighty Spain was under siege. A series of defeats both on land and on sea shook the very foundation of the Bourbon throne, then occupied by Phillip II. These losses would foreshadow the following century, a period which saw the dissolution and dismemberment of the once great empire.

The course that history eventually took in the Caribbean region was determined at the outset of the 17th century. In the 1590's, the English and the Dutch allied themselves against Spain. Their tactics proceeded along the methods introduced earlier: plunder and looting. In order to discourage the establishment of relations between the settlers and the seamen, the Spanish government absolutely forbade any trading between them. Violations of these regulations were often punished with death or exile to isolation. Nevertheless, many settlers risked being caught and thus a kind of black market industry gradually developed throughout the region.

Then in two separate treaties, with Britain in 1604 and with the Netherlands in 1609, Spain essentially bought off her enemies. The price? A concession that her enemies could freely settle the parts of America that Spain did not then occupy or control. These two agreements formed the legal basis for the ensuing colonization of the entire Western Hemisphere. For Spain it brought peace at little real cost. For England, Holland, France and even Austria, it brought the opportunity to settle anywhere in the New World not otherwise claimed by Spain or Portugal.

As we have seen, Spain and Portugal had their own agreement. These traditional enemies eventually got on rather well, despite their frequent squabbles and disputes. It seems that both governments saw that the advantages of cooperation greatly outweighed the fleeting glory of war. This cooperation produced the single most important change in the story of the Caribbean: The importation of negroes as slaves from Africa!

It was, after all, the Portuguese who first opened contacts with the west coast of Africa. Upon the loss or flight of the native Indian population in the region, they saw an opportunity to enslave the Africans. As it turned out, it was a prosperous undertaking, so much so that England and France followed suit. The Portuguese found that they could "buy" entire villages of people from African chiefs for a pittance. "If you can catch 'em, they're yours," was a cruel, but not uncommon response from many chiefs. In other instances slave traders hired mercenaries to hunt down and abduct as many "bodies" as they could, as long as they looked healthy. In any event, the toll it took on entire tribes was outrageous. It has been estimated that in the 17th century, four Africans died for each one that reached the islands. This sad beginning was to grow worse and even more tragic as the decades rolled on. The introduction of the slave trade to the Caribbean, where it all began, constitutes one of the saddest chapters in the story of mankind.

Meanwhile, France and England busily explored the Americas for profitable settlements. By 1610, the French were investing heavily in Canada and Florida. The British reached the central North American conti-nent in 1605 and founded the first settlement at Jamestown in 1607. Over the period of the following 20 years, both these countries grabbed unclaimed possessions in the West Indies. For the most part, antagonism between them and Spain remained constant, but not overboiling. The practice of pirate raids and black marketeering was begrudgingly acknowledged by all as a fact of life. As long as Spain could get most of her booty out, the region could remain calm. Then came the Dutch.

The role Holland played in the history of the West Indies cannot be properly understood without knowing a little Dutch history. For centuries, the territories that made up modern Netherlands were fought over by the French, English, Spanish, Germans and Italians. Finally, under Charles V, Spain gained the upper hand and retaliated brutally against the vanquished. The pro-British Protestant Dutch republicans, who eventually threw back Spanish controlled forces in Amsterdam, grew to bitterly resent Spain and its occupation.

In the early 1620's the Dutch West Indies Company was founded. This enterprise was not a sailing party of irresponsible sailors, but rather a well financed and organized profit making venture. It proposed to do what both the French and English failed to do before her: Crush the Spanish Main. Unlike her European neighbors Holland did not rely on naval strength alone. She had commercial and mercantile strengths to boot. In ten short years, the Dutch were ensconced in Venezuela and Brazil and on several islands off their coasts. From their headquarters in Curacao, the Dutch company quickly came to dominate shipping and slave trading. They made settlements on several other islands, primarily as port facilities, and they helped provide a protective shield for the

Spain :	Hispaniola, Cuba, Puerto Rico, Jamaica, St. Thomas, St. John, Tortuga, Trinidad.
France:	Martinique, St. Martin, Guadeloupe, St. Lucia.
England:	The Bahamas, Barbados, St. Kitts, Nevis, Montserrat, Antigua.
Holland:	Curacao, Saba, Aruba, Bonaire, St. Eustatius, St.Croix.

establishment of French and English settlements too.

By the first half of the 17th century the rival nations claimed the islands in the figure below.

In many instances, these claims were contested by one or more of the others. For example, the Dutch claimed St. Martin, the French claimed Montserrat and the British claimed almost anything they possibly could. As we shall see, possession of most of the islands changed hands numerous times.

It must be remembered that these claims were to the islands themselves, and entirely separate from their continental claims. The Dutch, for example ,made progress settling the interior of Guiana, despite its tropical perils. The British laid claim to northwestern Honduras and subsequently, a large portion of Guiana too. As we have seen, the British and French were also settling North America during this period. Try as they did, the warring parties could not dislodge Spain and Portugal from their measurably large colonies in South and Central America.

As the European powers gradually recognized the

sheer size and potential of their American possessions, the business of organizing and managing expeditions became more polished. The nobility were awarded huge land grants by their monarchs. In return, they invested their money and resources into settling and colonizing these areas. They encouraged peoples of diverse trades with incentives to move to the islands and start their lives anew. In this new era, the first towns and farms were established throughout the region that was not first settled by the Spaniards. The tales that grew out of this period of human ingenuity and accomplishment are still in circulation in the quiet outer reaches of the Caribbean. The current names of towns and hills, bays and estates, for the most part owe their origins to these first settlers.

But the difficulties that these courageous settlers experienced cannot be discounted. The very nature of the times and great distances involved made hardships inevinable. The role that storms and hurricanes played the region is well documented. They frequently left death and destruction in their wake. The effects of drought and disease were equally crippling. Being cut off from the outside world, except by the occasional rat infested ship, illness, epidemics and malnutrition diminished the number of settlers, slaves and natives through the period of colonization of the West Indies. Bloody battles with the Carib Indians of the islands were not uncommon either. In many instances, the native tribes completely wiped out settlements and killed all the Europeans in sight. Of course, this frequently brought retaliation and almost certain re-settlement with fortifications. The same fate met the settlers of North America too. The only difference being that on the continent, the natives tribes had room to maneuver and retreat. By contrast, the natives of the islands had nowhere to go. Thus they tended to stand and fight. This sad fact was responsible for the death of the last native Indian races. To the extent that some natives were subjugated or surrendered, they were usually treated as laborers and servants. It was ,after all, their loss that caused the Europeans to import slaves from Africa.

For the Europeans it was an economic windfall; for the blacks, it was an unmitigated catastrophe. The horrors of the "middle passage" were separate and distinct from the cruelties of slavery itself. The major slave traders were the Portuguese and the English. The French and the Dutch however, also participated in it, but to a lesser degree. Spain ostensibly rejected the commerce of human bondage, but Spanish colonies did indeed supply and trade black slaves. The conditions which the blacks were subjected to during the three to four week voyage can only be described as barbaric. Chained and bound, they were thrown together below deck like beans in a pot. Food and water were strictly rationed and silence was always the order from above.

One such African, captured when he was 21 years old, described the conditions on a typical Caribbean-bound slave trading ship :

"The stench of the hold was so intolerably loathsome that it was dangerous to remain there for any length of time...The closeness of the place and the heat of the climate, added to the number in the ship, which was so crowded that each had scarcely room to turn himself, almost suffocated us. This produced copious perspira-tions, so that the air soon became unfit for respiration from a variety of loathsome smells, and brought on a sickness among the slaves of which many died...This wretched situation was again aggravated by the galling of the chains and the filth of the necessary tubs, into which the children often fell and almost drowned. The shrieks of the women and the groans of the dying rendered the whole a scene of horror almost inconceivable..."

Upon arrival in port, the slaves were separated and auctioned off. Families were divided and tribal traditions were banned. Slaves were ordered to work fields, build roads and buildings, fish or mine for gold and silver. Female slaves and children were employed as servants and plantation hands. A British Commission summed up the consequences many years later as follows:

"When the Africans were introduced into the West Indies as slave labor, no attempt was made to substitute any kind of social organization or moral standard for the somewhat elaborate tribal codes of the areas whence they were brought. The benefits of education

and the institution of marriage were alike discouraged, and on emancipation a large number of persons were left to shift for themselve without the support of traditions of self-help or mutual co-operation...The work of the religious bodie during this period served to win for the churches and religion a special place in the hearts and lives of the people. In developing education in particular the religious bodies have played a noteworthy part. But they were unable to exert more than a limited influence on either the moral standards or the social conditions of the community."

The lasting influence of the Catholic Church in the region cannot be overlooked. Earlier, we learned of the respect both Spain and Portugal paid to the church in exchange for Papal blessings and favors. In the New World, the Jesuits and other missionaries worked endlessly to establish faith and civil discipline in the hearts and minds of the settlers. In other instances, the missionaries brought religion directly to the natives, who accepted it without fear. These works raised the ire of mercantile interests. As one might expect, the rich shippers and slave traders had more influence and power than the Jesuits. Their contribution to life and society in the islands and on the continents was nevertheless significant. In subsequent years, the Protestants also made lasting contributions to the area. For the most part, the churches, seminaries and schools founded in that day still exist and prosper today. In this regard, their mission must be considered an overwhelming success.

In the second half of the 17th century, the agricultural output of the Caribbean possessions rose rapidly. Large plantations of cotton, tobacco and most importantly, sugar, supplied European ports in plentiful amounts. Among the other crops that were introduced were coffee, citrus fruits, grapes, herbs for spices, tomatoes, berries, pineapple, beets, carrots, greens of all kinds and beans of all flavors. Of course, some crops grew better than others. Many which were introduced became failures. As we shall see, the mild and arid soil of the West Indies always proved problematical.

There was always a demand for tough minded Europeans to settle in the islands. The conquest of the New

World took its toll on them too. When in Europe, principally England and then Germany, religious strife rose, Protestant dissenters bravely settled the Americas. These were the first pilgrims that we read about in school as children. Their lives were not easy in their new home. The sacrifices these founders made in the hope of achieving spiritual and financial prosperity are truly remarkable.

Due to their employment of slaves, large estate owners had an obvious economic advantage over the small family farmer. As a general rule, smaller farmers served the needs of the local communities and sailors. They saw no part of the wealth that their feudal lords were extracting from the land and sea. The disparity of income between the average settler and titled landlord quickly produced a class system along traditional European lines. For every success story in the West Indies there were a hundred tales of failure. The vanquished and disgraced had little hope of survival except by illegal means. These they often chose.

From the start of the Spanish conquest, ships carrying valuable cargo sailed back and forth over the Atlantic Ocean and Caribbean Sea, linking the Old and New Worlds together. Shipwrecks were common, especially within the coral and sand hazards of the expansive Bahama Islands which served as the gateway between Atlantic and Caribbean waters. Stories have been told of how desperate settlers lured unsuspecting ships onto the rocks by the use of false beacons. This problem was partially solved by the construction of regular lighthouses in the 19th century. In the 17th, however, such tactics often meant disaster. In the wake of the wreck, islanders would hurriedly loot everything of value they could find. Sometimes their antics brought huge rewards, but to an isolated settler, anything new would do. On many of the Caribbean islands, income from wrecking and cargo salvaging far outpaced that from farming.

Controversy inevitably arose as a result. Spain especially objected to these practices, for she was the largest victim. The Spanish governors of Havana and Santo Domingo never hesitated to plunder a town or two in response to wrecking activities. These pressures, together with the proliferation of the black marketeering and the general rise in competition for wealth, combined to produce one of the most interesting aspects of the Caribbean story: Pirates.

As described earlier, the warring European nations actively supported the use of mercenaries against each other. When, from time to time, relative calm was established under British-Dutch-Spanish enforced treaties, the privateers became outright pirates. As such, they became free to attack any ship they could catch. Soon, pirates and buccaneers, so named for their tradition of smoking meat in open air coal pits, roamed the islands like bulls in a pasture. While the major trading companies relied on large armadas to protect their cargo filled

Sir Henry Morgan
(1635-1688)
A pirate who subsequently became the Governor of Jamaica, Morgan is reputed to have been the first slave trader in the West Indies.

ships, the pirates relied on speed and mobility. They were masters at the art of hit-and-run sailing. They regularly controlled many small cays and coves where they hid out and divided their ill-gotten gains.

The many small islands of the Bahamas and Lesser Antilles were favorite pirate hangouts.. They would plunder and raze towns at random. Their only saving grace is that they didn't regularly occupy them, preferring the open sea for their safety. Many a depressed settler joined their ranks in hope of gaining wealth and glory. They succumbed to the romantic appeal of adventure and the pirate's "code of honor", a violation of which meant certain death. Among those that left their reputations to legend were Sir Henry Morgan, Calico Jack Rackham, Edward "Blackbeard" Teach, Benjamin Horngold, Stede Bonnet and the two rugged female pirates, Anne Bonnay and Mary Read.

The pirates' favorite bases of operation were from Nassau, Tobago, French controlled Hispaniola, San Juan and elsewhere. In 1692 the main pirate port of Port Royal on the southern peninsula of Jamaica was wiped out by an earthquake and resulting tidal wave. It scattered the survivors throughout the West Indies and numerous small bands of criminals resulted. Meantime, on the European controlled isles, land-based maroon buccaneers lived and hid in the woods. They struck at settlements, took hostages and provisions and frequently obtained ransom in return. Their way of life created a curious folklore filled with cunning and adventure. Even as the shores and coastal towns of the West Indies expanded, their interiors and mountain valleys contained their own societies of Indians, runaway slaves and desperados. These groups lived together, but remained separate from each other. From this stock grew the citizens of the islands, supplemented over the years by slaves, fortune hunters, adventure seekers and finally, tourists.

The foundation upon which the history of the Caribbean Islands rests has been laid out for you. As was stated in the Introduction, the similarity of experience which these islands shared brought them together as "one people out of many". These similarities are inbred in their language, culture, customs and traditions. It extends to art and music and encompasses dancing, crafts, shipbuilding and cooking. But each island group actually is unique. The haphazard manner in which the West Indies were settled, combined with the throes of frequent upheaval, produced many separate peoples with their own separate stories.

Thus, in the interest of getting you better acquainted with the particulars, what follows are short descriptive chronologies of each of the significant islands and isle groups of the Caribbean Sea. Enjoy them as you enjoy your vacation.

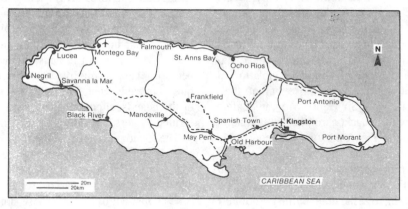

Jamaica

he island of Jamaica was sighted by Columbus on his second voyage to the New World in May, 1494. There he encountered friendly Arawak natives and presented them with gifts. An estimate of their population at that time ranges from 40,000 to 60,000. After a period of skepticism, the Arawaks began to trust the Spaniards and bartered for goods with them. After a few days, Columbus abruptly sailed away having found no evidence of gold. Before he left, however, he claimed the island a Spanish possession and renamed it St. Jago.

For the next ten years, the Arawaks of Jamaica lived free of Spanish interference. But on his fourth voyage to the New World, Columbus and his crew returned to the island for the purpose of testing its soil and vegetation. This time, their rotting, worm-infested ships sank into the mud in what has come to be called St. Ann's

Bay on the southern coast of the oblong island. Columbus, his son, his brother and about 160 others, were thus stranded on Jamaica in 1503. Their isolation was filled with great hardships and human tragedies. Famine, disease and mutiny spread among them while the Arawaks chose to keep their distance. Finally, after about a year, the desperate survivors were rescued and taken to Hispaniola. One can understand why they were unwilling to return.

It was not until 1510 that the first planned settlement of Jamaica was attempted. In that year, Captain Juan de Esquivel was appointed governor and charged with the responsibility of charting and colonizing the island "for the benefit of the Spanish Crown". The first settlement at *Sevilla la Nueva* on "New Seville" on St. Ann's Bay was quickly abandoned in favor of a new site in the south which became present day "Spanish Town." In sub-

Jamaica's national emblem and motto.

sequent years, several other towns were established around the island's exterior.

The tremendous amount of physical labor required to turn a desolate sea shore into a functioning town and fort cannot be underestimated. Not only was forest clearing and new construction required, but farms had to be established to supply food for the settlers. The demand for labor prompted the Spaniards to capture and enslave the Arawaks. In exchange for their freedom, the natives were promised food, protection and conversion to Christianity. The Spaniards thought they were being very generous but the Arawaks felt differently. Armed conflicts soon arose and Jamaica's peaceful green hills quickly became one great battlefield. Accordingly, Jamaica as a Spanish colony was largely a failure. Its main purpose was to serve as a seaport for Spanish commerce.

As time passed, more crops were introduced. Pig and cattle farming became mainstays on the island. The first slaves from Africa were imported in 1517 to replace the dying Arawaks. No serious attempt was made in exploring the island's interior or in developing its natural resources. Jamaica's plentiful supplies of clear water from her countless fresh mountain springs became the island's chief attraction and saving feature. Jamaican spring water was said to produce the sweetest rum.

By the year 1600, about a dozen small settlements had been founded. Jamaica's difficult terrain and relative distance from other islands served to individualize each town's people and the products they offered for sale as provisions. However, a string of ineffective governors, combined with a lack of support from Spain or the other New World settlements, gradually weakened her economy and caused many to flee to Cuba, Hispaniola and elsewhere.

As we have already learned, other Europeans sailed into the picture at the start of the 17th century. After a botched attempt to conquer Santo Domingo in 1654, a British expedition turned to Jamaica as a consolation prize. After about a year of warfare in appalling conditions, they successfully ousted the Spaniards and claimed all of Jamaica from 1655 onwards. For many years thereafter, Spaniards and slaves who had escaped into the interior offered token resistance, but they were never strong enough to discourage the anxious English army and navy. A final Spanish attempt to reconquer the island was repulsed in 1658. Jamaica was formally ceded to Britain under the Treaty of Madrid in 1670.

The British quickly populated the island and transformed it into their main base for attacking Spanish ships. Over the next 40 years, more than 12,000 Europeans arrived on Jamaica. Those who came were loyal farmers and fishermen, and among them came the first Anglican missionaries in the New World. Many others were sent involuntarily, either because they were religious outcasts, furloughed convicts or conquered Irish and Scots. Gradually, and despite endless obstacles, including a full-scale rebellion, the British established their presence on most of the island. Under the capable leadership of Colonel Edward D Oyley, they established plantations of banana, sugar, tobacco, cocoa, and pineapple. Fortifications were erected and new towns were established in good order. Thanks to a series of competent governorships, the island enjoyed a civil administration unequaled anywhere else in the West Indies.

The relative success of her products encouraged the British to import more and more slaves. By 1680, the Negroes (as they were called) had become the majority on the island. The appalling conditions in which they were forced to live and work have already been described. It, therefore, was not uncommon for slaves to run away into Jamaica's rugged interior and in many cases, join up with former Spanish holdouts. These interior dwellers took the name "Maroons" from the Spanish word cimarron meaning beast. Relentlessly, they continued to raid British towns for food and supplies for 200 years before they gradually melted into Jamaican society. Over that period of time Jamaica enjoyed a level of colonial success which was rare in the Caribbean. With the loss of the North American colonies in 1776, British interests in the region were channeled back to the West Indies, where it has continued its rule until today.

Some of the highlights of Jamaica's history are worthy of notation. At the top of the list is the rise of piracy from Jamaica's southern peninsula of Port Royal. So strong were its participants that if it were not for the earthquake and tidal wave of 1692, the pirates might have taken over the entire island. In the wake of the confusion following the quake, the French landed an expeditionary force on Jamaica's eastern end in 1697. Terrible fighting followed, which saw the destruction of numerous farms and sugar mills. When they finally left, the French carried off everything they could, including more than one thousand slaves. This attack was the last real battle fought on Jamaican soil. Following the Treaty of Utrecht in 1713, Jamaica became England's main slave market in the West Indies. This brought Spanish, Portuguese and Dutch commerce to the island. The resulting prosperity enticed new pirate bands. In 1720, Spanish Town hosted a great pirate trial in which "Calico" Jack Rackham was convicted and hanged. His remains were displayed in an iron frame as a warning to others. The sunny islet where they hung him is still called Rackham's Cay.

In the mid 18th century, the problem of illegal trading reared its ugly head. At that time ships were routinely intercepted by the Spaniards and Portuguese for purpose of inspections. These actions angered the British especially. Disputes arose over what was and what was not permissible cargo. These incidents gradually escalated into a full scale war. The British and Dutch teamed up against Spain and Portugal's ally, France. By 1763, Spain and France had lost numerous possessions and more importantly, their prestige in the region.

A hurricane in the fall of 1780 caused considerable damage to eastern Jamaica and resulting fires destroyed much of her agriculture. During that period, all of Jamaica's resources were strained to aid the British war effort on the continent. Spain and France contented themselves by striking back at weakened British possessions. Finally, a siege of Jamaica was beaten back by Admiral George Rodney in a great sea confrontation called the Battle of the Saints in April 1782. The British bestowed upon Rodney the title of "Lord" and gave him a pension and land grant. Today, a memorial statue of Lord Rodney dominates the public square in Spanish Town, flanked by two decorous captured French cannons.

As sugar plantations dominated the economy, the British saw fit to develop a part of the plains of Liguanea, near the sea. The settlement known as King's Town grew and prospered. In 1872, Kingston (as the town came to be called) became the headquarters of the British colonial administration. The political authority of the island consisted of a governor appointed by the Crown, who along with a local council of landlords carried out executive powers. A legislative House of Assembly had been authorized back in 1661, but it was not formally established until 1672. To a very large extent, Jamaica enjoyed autonomy during its formative years, the British Parliament being busy with other matters both at home and abroad. Though her largest landlords were absentee owners, their agents on the island saw to it that their interests yielded satisfactory returns.

But Jamaica's social structure was terribly fragmented. The comparative wealth enjoyed by a few caused wide resentment. The anger of the white settlers was usually bought off with concessions, but the anger of the Blacks was treated as an act of insurrection. Thus, beginning in the 17th century and continuing through the establishment of Jamaican independence in 1962, a series of fateful revolts and uprisings rocked the island. The first was known as Tacky's Rebellion of 1760. What started as a local dispute in the parish of St. Mary's, spread throughout the island within a month. Tacky and his comrades conducted many raids and killed numerous farmers and government officials. After a giant manhunt in which the British even hired the Maroons as allies, Tacky was shot dead; his supporters committed suicide rather than be taken alive. During Christmas in 1831, an uprising in St. James parish proved that the end of the slave trade 24 years before hardly changed a thing. Led by "Daddy" Samuel Sharpe, a Baptist minister, the revolt caused considerable destruction and upheaval. The retaliatory measures the estate owners took against their slaves can only be described as thoughtless and cruel.

Stories of this kind did not end with the abolition of slavery in 1838. Rather, due to the inevitable decline in

A typical poster announcing a slave auction.

Jamaica's economy, the situation grew much worse. Poverty and pestilence were rampant and little aid from England was forthcoming. Attempts to transport indentured labor from India and China only complicated matters. Suddenly, in October 1865, the most dramatic revolt erupted spontaneously. Known as the Morant Bay Rebellion, the entire island quickly turned to chaos. The leader of the revolt was an ex-slave from St. Thomas parish named Paul Bogle, who is a present day national hero. The riots were apparently sparked by a magistrate's ruling in a land dispute. Pleas to Governor Edward Eyre fell on deaf ears. The ensuing violence caused hundreds of deaths and the loss of an entire season's harvests.

The rebellion was crushed by brute force. More than 430 black dissidents, including Bogle and his brother were executed and a thousand more were flogged and ordered to work in chain gangs. The rebellion caused immense destruction. Entire towns were razed and more than 1,200 homes were burned to the ground. For the Blacks, emancipation was just a word, freedom, a dream.

The uprising compelled the island Assembly to vote in favor of Crown Colony status. This act effectively gave control of the island's affairs to the Parliament in London. The move was made in the hope that it would calm passions and result in more British aid. These hopes were partially realized in the latter part of the 19th century, the period in which the modern state of Jamaica began to take shape. The government formed a post office, a new court system and local constabularies. The first schools and medical clinics were set up in each of Jamaica's frontier districts. The contributions of the Anglican Church were substantial. Streets were cleared of debris, a railroad was established and town buildings and houses were built anew. In 1879, the Instititute of Jamaica was founded to encourage the study of literature, science and the arts.

By the turn of the century, the Jamaican economy had developed a pattern different from the slave-based sugar plantation models elsewhere in the West Indies. Not only did she produce a greater variety of agricultural products, but a significant percentage was grown by independent peasant farmers rather than on large estates. This relative "agricultural pluralism" did not, however, carry over into political power. For two centuries, the government had been run in an authoritarian manner by the governor and his advisory council. Voting rights were highly restrictive and one could not seek election to the assembly unless he was a substantial land owner himself. Thus, old landed interests based primarily in England had effective control over Jamaica's government and economy. The disparity in Jamaica was made glaringly evident after the great earthquake of 1907. The devastation it caused killed thousands and inflicted great damage everywhere. The relief effort, however, was entirely controlled by government officials who saw to commercial interests before those of the people.

With the onset of the world depression in the 1930's, the cause of the island's black majority finally came to be heard. Mass poverty and unemployment naturally fueled resentment toward the old order. Moreover, segregation and neglect for social services were responsible for terrible inequities between black and white citizens.

In the face of discontent, the black majority slowly began to mobilize. In the period between the world wars, blacks had begun to form trade unions, schools, newspapers and political clubs which gave rise to political aspirations. Among those who best expressed the aspirations of the people was Marcus Garvey, one of Jamaica's most enigmatic heroes.* His aim of uniting all black peoples of the world was, however, deemed highly suspect by London.

Under the weight of these pressures, Jamaican society continued to disintegrate. Events reached their crest during the summer of 1938, when widespread violence and disruption culminated with the establishment of the first majority political party, the People's National Party (PNP) under socialist lawyer Norman Manley. Though his message was actually quite moderate, Manley had the enthusiastic support of the black community, which made up about ninety percent of Jamaica's population

*The Rastafari Brotherhood, which in 1935 hailed Ethiopia's Emperor Haile Selassie as their mystic leader, continue to testify to the lasting contribution of Garvey in Jamaica.

of 1.25 million.

In 1942, labor leader Alexander Bustamante was released from prison where he had been sent for inciting rebellion. His popularity and fatherly image propelled him into forming the Jamaica Labor Party (JLP). Both leaders pressed not only for economic reform, but for political reform too. With the election of 1944, both parties received substantial support and elected an equal number of representatives to the assembly. The conservative Jamaican Democratic Party, formed by wealthy landowners and businesses failed to win a single seat. This prompted the Parliament in London to agree to a new constitution. The modified system was a landmark victory for the people, who were granted civil rights, including universal adult suffrage. For the next quarter of a century, Manley and Bustamante occupied the center of Jamaican political affairs. Their contributions to the cause of Jamaican liberty and independence are self-evident and enduring.

The 1950's were a watershed in Jamaican history. Several new developmental schemes in agriculture and industry were commenced. The mining of bauxite from the country's interior increased rapidly, as did a rise in tourism.* The economy made impressive gains and social stability appeared to revive at last. In 1954, self-government from England was achieved. With the exception of defense and international affairs, Jamaica became ruled entirely by her own representatives. In an attempt to forestall any further deterioration of her empire, the British encouraged the establishment of an independent West Indies Federation in 1958. But in Jamaica it was too late. The idea of Jamaica joining a federal union with islands over a thousand miles away angered many. A referendum was held in 1961 and the idea was soundly rejected. Moreover, Manley's PNP, which had been lukewarm to the idea was ousted by Bustamante's JLP, which vehemently rejected it.

Negotiations between Britain and the JLP began immediately. By February 1962 an agreement on a new constitution was reached and Jamaica's Independence

*Bauxite is the main ore in aluminum.

Day was set for August 6, 1962. Two weeks of celebration followed and Bustamante became Jamaica's first prime minister. In 1963, Jamaica became the 109th nation of the United Nations. The moderate JLP remained in power until the elections of 1972 when Michael Manley, Norman's energetic trade unionist son, became the new PNP prime minister. He advocated a policy of Democratic Socialism which soon aggravated many American business interests. The rising disillusionment which his policy of reform caused cost the PNP the election of 1980. Once again the JLP was returned to leadership, this time under the former minister of development, Edward Seaga. His close alliance with the administration of U.S. President Ronald Reagan brought significant new investments into Jamaica's ailing economy.

Today, Jamaica stands at the crossroads in the Caribbean basin. The expansion of industry and tourism in the face of a rising population and demand for services is a characteristic way of life in the region. The yearning for progress and development remains high throughout the islands. Jamaica's fortunes are greatly enhanced by her strong democratic character and institutions, and her mixture of ethnic groups who learned to live together. Jamaica's national motto "One People Out of Many" is particularly fitting in light of her unusual and tumultuous history.

uerto Rico and the Virgin Islands were discovered by Columbus in November, 1493 on his second voyage to the New World. He claimed the larger island for Spain and renamed it San Juan de Bautista (St. John the Baptist). The first settlement was commenced by Spanish Captain Juan Ponce de Leon, who upon his arrival supposedly exclaimed, "que puerto rico" or "what a rich port" - and the name survived. The main settlement was named San Juan in 1521 and has served as the capital city ever since.

Due to its modest gold mining prospects and mountainous terrain, Puerto Rico under Spain's rule remained essentially undeveloped. Its main purpose, due to its strategic position at the entrance of the Caribbean Sea, was as a defensive base to protect the rich neighboring island of Hispaniola. As elsewhere in the West Indies, Spain enslaved the native Arawaks, and by 1518 began buying slaves from Africa. Within 50 years, the sociable coastal natives had mostly died out, leaving the more fierce Carib natives in the interior. The Carib, along with runaway slaves, plundered and plagued the poor island settlements for the next 200 years. The relatively small population of the island inhibited the rise of spontaneous upheavals and criminal activity. Gradually, emigration and intermarriage lessened the social tensions that existed elsewhere on the islands of the Caribbean Sea.

The Puerto Rican economy developed a keen sensitivity to seagoing commerce. Beginning in the 1520's her large plantations supplied sugar, cotton, ginger, tobacco and coffee to European markets. Her relative prosperity and proximity to Hispaniola prompted the British to attempt several attacks, starting in 1595. San Juan was occupied in 1598 for three months, but British forces withdrew due to an outbreak of smallpox. The Dutch attempted to capture San Juan in 1625. However, this attack was also repulsed by the Spanish settlers, but only after the city was once again looted and burned to the ground. Spanish fortifications were rebuilt and Puerto Rico became richly supported by a tax on Mexico until that country won its independence from Spain in 1810. Thus, Puerto Rico enjoyed a measure of tranquility uncommon during the 17th and 18th centuries.

Puerto Rico's first census, taken in 1765, revealed a population of 45,000 of whom roughly one half were slaves and convict laborers. When thereafter her ports were opened for foreign trade, a wave of immigrants arrived from Spanish colonies in South and Central America, most of which were in revolt. In 1807 the first daily newspaper *La Gazeta* (The Gazette) began publishing and Puerto Rico was accorded representation in the ruling Spanish Caribbean Council. By 1832, the population had swelled to 330,000 and there were more than 300 towns established throughout the island.

Despite several small instances of armed resistance against Spanish rule in the mid-1800's, Puerto Rico remained comparatively pacified. In 1869, Puerto Rico was removed from colony status and made a province of Spain. Slavery was abolished by 1873. The Catholic Church had established several major missions in Puerto Rico and the influence of Jesuit missionaries on the island was particularly strong. Then in 1876, due to continued insistence by the Puerto Ricans themselves, Spain passed a law inviting Puerto Rico to be represented in the legislature of Madrid. This move fueled the debate on the future of the island. On the one side were the conservative forces who favored the status quo. On the other were Puerto Rican nationalists who demanded complete independence. Finally in 1897, a compromise was reached and Puerto Rico became an "autonomous community associated with Spain." This brought the people" home rule "for the first time, long before any other colony in the West Indies.

But Puerto Rico's autonomy from Spain was to be short-lived. In 1898 the U.S.S. Maine was docked in Havana Harbor. It mysteriously exploded killing 260 U.S. sailors. Despite Puerto Rico's apology, the U.S. declared war on Spain. A small U.S. fleet landed at Puerto Rico's southern coastal port of Guancia on July

25th. After a few light skirmishes, the Spanish governor capitulated in fear. When the Treaty of Paris was signed on December 10, 1898, Spain had ceded Puerto Rico, Cuba, the Philippines and Guam to the U.S. Needless to say, it was a humiliating defeat for the once powerful Spain.

For the next two years, U.S. military rule prevailed and modest efforts were made to improve the physical infrastructure of the island. In 1899, municipal elections were held and it was apparent that most Puerto Ricans favored statehood. Their hopes were extinguished a year later when the U.S. Congress enacted a law establishing a new civil administration on the island. The law provided for the appointment of a governor and the upper chamber of a bicameral legislature of which the lower chamber was to be popularly elected. The law provided for the establishment of an independent judiciary as well. All laws and actions were, however, subject to approval from Washington. Puerto Rico was exempted from paying any U.S. taxes and free trade was established to stimulate the island's economy. However, Puerto Rico's legal status remained unaddressed.

Then, as opposition to these measures increased, the U.S. Congress passed a new law (Jones Act of 1917) awarding U.S. citizenship to all Puerto Ricans and amending some of the more restrictive provisions of the earlier measure. In 1929, Theodore Roosevelt Jr. became governor. His popularity and energetic style soothed the prevailing tensions many were feeling. He advocated a program for new elections, economic development, cultural protection and enhanced political liberties.

The violence and turmoil that swept the Caribbean during the 1930's did not exclude Puerto Rico. The rise of a paramilitary organization called the Nationalist Party led to public protests and riots. One incident in the large town of Ponce on Palm Sunday 1937 caused the deaths of eleven citizens and injury to over one hundred others. Inaction on the part of the U.S. Congress only strengthened the position of separatist radicals.

In 1940, the newly formed Popular Democratic Party (PDP) won control of the legislature. Economic reform, not political indulgence, was its chief promise to the people. After the civil unrest and the crippling effects of two hurricanes (1938 and 1942), the island was in need of a shot in the arm. Led by Luis Munoz Marin, the PDP undertook a number of important proposals called Operation Bootstrap. Among the changes offered was the establishment of the Puerto Rico Planning Board, the Economic Development Association and a national governmental bank. These agencies spearheaded moves to expand public utilities, establish water, sewage and sanitation systems and helped develop transportation by road and rail alike. These measures attracted U.S. capital for the expansion of industry and tourism.

In 1947, Puerto Rico was given the power to elect her own governor and Munoz Marin won by a landslide the following year. Under pressure to finally determine Puerto Rico's legal status with the U.S., a constitution was adopted which declared Puerto Rico a commonwealth, under U.S. protection. On July 25, 1952, a referendum overwhelmingly supported this designation and so Puerto Rico remains to this day.

The PDP continued to rule until 1968, when the candidate for the opposing New Progressive Party, led by Luis Ferre, gained enough support to take over the legislature and governorship. Since then, power has been alternately shared by both parties in what are commonly considered fair and robust elections.

Puerto Rico has yet to recover from the long period in which she faced a real identity crisis. The nationalist movement, while considerably weakened, is by no means dead. The relative stability the island has achieved due to tourism and U.S. government aid has fostered the growth of cultural and educational institutions. The problems that remain: unemployment, inflation and overpopulation, are endemic to the region, but Puerto Rico's relationship to the U.S. makes such problems a bit more manageable than those of her Caribbean cousins.

The Virgin Islands of the U.S. and Great Britain shared a similar heritage to that of Puerto Rico, but with a few important differences. Their comparatively tiny size lessened their geographic or economic importance until the rise of Caribbean tourism in the 1950's.

The U.S. possessions in the region are the three main

islands east of Puerto Rico. They are St. Croix (which Columbus named Santa Cruz), St. John and St. Thomas.

The first settlement activity took place in St. Croix in the early 17th century. At that time, France, England and Holland were anxious to establish possessions in the West Indies. Their intermittent rivalry with Spain made such possessions a military must. By 1625, both the French and the British claimed St. Croix. Rather than fight for control, the two nations established separate towns and farms to serve their fleets. France soon disclaimed its settlements after both Dutch and Spanish attacks discouraged French settlers from remaining. By 1650 only a few English settlements remained.

But Spain soon toppled the English too. Fearful that the British fleet was about to attack Santo Domingo, the island was evacuated except for a few old slaves and little or no activity was permitted on the island. During the next two years, the French fought their way back to St. Croix and established several settlements on the north shore. Then in 1653 ,the French government ceded the island to the Knights of Malta, an ancient brotherhood who had lost considerable wealth at the hands of the Spaniards and British in Europe. The brotherhood dated back to the crusades of the Middle Ages and accepted the island as a compromise of their claim on the French government. Within ten years, however, France bought St. Croix back. From that point on, France occupied the island for its strategic location, but for little else.

As described earlier in this book, the major European powers of Spain, Portugal, England, France and Holland all actively pursued policies of exploitation in the West Indies. In the 1660's Denmark also decided to partake of the riches of the region. Rather than proceed in the fashion of the day, namely pillage and plunder, the Danes claimed unwanted and deserted islands. In 1666 they landed at St. Thomas and later in St. John, which are respectively only 28 and 20 square miles in size.

The Danes intended to establish Spanish-style plantations for their own markets. To this end they methodically divided the land and granted individual estates to willing speculators. The rocky soil, coupled with a lack of irrigation, however, dashed these hopes. By 1730, the two islands were serving the commercial shipping industry with meat and vegetables. The population of the islands remained sparse, but remarkably diverse. Slaves were imported but not in large numbers. Many Danes fled the island while others arrived in earnest. In 1733, Denmark successfully negotiated the purchase of St. Croix from France.

The pirate era did not leave any of the islands undisturbed. Their location in the heart of the Caribbean, between the Bahamas and the Greater Antilles made St. Croix and St. John favorite pirate hide-a-ways. Their ill-gotten rewards soon proved so large that the Danish government entered into secret leases with the pirates in exchange for a share of their takings. The benign Danish rule lasted another 175 years. In 1776, the Danish government became the first to salute the American flag from Fort Frederick in St. Croix. Slavery was formally abolished in 1848 and the islanders lived quietly until the dawn of the 20th century. The beautiful farm houses and colorful buildings of the main towns, and the many patios and plazas of the rural area remain a testament to Danish

Harvest of Sugar Cane.

influence.

In 1917, the U.S. government purchased the Danish Virgin Islands for $25 million. Two reasons have been offered: First, to provide a naval base for the defense of the Panama Canal; second, to discourage Imperial Germany from shipping weapons to the raging Mexican civil war. In any event, the purchase was consummated through bipartisan support in Washington.

Since that time, the U.S. Virgin Islands have enjoyed benefits not found elsewhere in the region. Investment and development have brought to these islands the highest per capita income in the Caribbean. Apart from U.S. Navy installations, the greatest boost to their economy has been tourism. St. Thomas, for example, is the West Indies' most popular cruise port-of-call. Moreover, duty-free shopping has resulted in substantial retail development in her capital city, Charlotte Amalie (pronounced Ah-mah-lhy). The islands elect their own governor and legislative branches and enjoy effective self-rule. The beauty, location and many attractions of the U.S. Virgin Islands will undoubtedly assure their place as "the favor-ite gems" of the Caribbean.

By contrast, the British Virgin Islands, a neighboring group of smaller isles, shared a history closer to that of other Leeward Islands such as Antigua, Montserrat and St. Kitts. Since they are very small and hilly, they never ranked on the scale of commercial importance. Out of a total of 40 islands, 15 are presently inhabited. Tortola is the largest and most important of the group, yet its capital city, Road Town, only has about 3,000 residents.

Tortola was first settled by the English in the 1620's. It was granted a royal charter by George III in 1773. The exact nature of the grant was never spelled out and so the settlers grabbed as many neighboring islands they as could. What little historical development that took place was confined to the raising of livestock and fishing. The other islands were intermittently occupied by the French and then by buccaneers. In 1666, France ceded them to England by treaty. The islands were ruled jointly with the other Leewards until 1956, when the British government joined them to the West Indies Federation. But the British Virgin Islands rejected the move and have, since then, chosen to remain a full crown colony. Since the 1970's, the islands have benefited greatly from the rise in tourism.

Since it is rare that one actually has the opportunity to learn the names of the British Virgin Islands, a list in order of population is as follows: Tortola, Virgin Gorda, Anegada, Jost Van Dyke, Beef Island, Guana Island and Great Camanoe.

British Virgin Islands

U.S. Virgin Islands

Puerto Rico

Isla Desecheo and
Isla Mona are not shown.

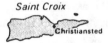

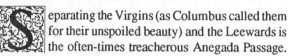

Separating the Virgins (as Columbus called them for their unspoiled beauty) and the Leewards is the often-times treacherous Anegada Passage. The northernmost island is Anguilla which remains a British colony. It is a small island (35 square miles) and is never more than three miles wide. Its history is uneventful except in the latter half of the 20th century when it defiantly ceded from a tiny confederation with its neighbors to the south, St. Kitts and Nevis. So anxious were the British that they sent a naval squadron and dropped Royal Marines in via parachute. The rebellion culminated in the dissolution of the association in 1980. Its 6,500 citizens are mostly poor and make their living by fishing, gold panning, boat crafting and raising livestock.

St. Kitts-Nevis became fully independent on September 18, 1983, but chose to remain within the British Commonwealth of Nations. Columbus landed on St. Kitts in 1493 and named it St. Christopher, its official name until independence was achieved. It became the first permanent English settlement in the West Indies. By 1650 it was called the "mother colony" because it served as a launching base for numerous other colonizing groups. Nevis (pronounced Nee-vis) was claimed by England as early as 1628 and became a weigh station for her larger neighbors to the north. The French also coveted St. Christopher and engaged in countless battles with the British over the next 150 years. The territorial dispute was finally resolved in the same document that settled the American Revolutionary War, the Treaty of Versailles of 1783.

Nevis is the birthplace of the famous American revolutionary Alexander Hamilton. An orphan by age 11, he went to the Danish Virgin Islands to live with a maternal aunt. His lucid newspaper account of a hurricane in St. Croix came to the attention of the local governor. By age 15, the boy's talents were clear enough to see. He was therefore sent to Boston for "a proper education." He went on to become General Washington's aide-de-camp and distinguished himself in the victory of Yorktown. After the war he became a noted lawyer in New York and then a Congressman and finally the first Secretary of the Treasury of the U.S. He was killed in a celebrated duel with his rival Aaron Burr in 1804. The house of Hamilton's birth has been fully restored and can be visited in Charleston, Nevis' main town.

Spain's initial claim to the Leeward Islands was forfeited by lack of possession. A British company from Ireland settled Montserrat in 1632, primarily as a fishing colony. For a time, the island operated as a penal colony for dissident Irish nationalists. The French and the buccaneers likewise seized the island, but they too yielded to British control in 1666. Today it remains a colony.

The island was named by Columbus in honor of the seminary in Spain at Montserrat. Its 37 square miles of mountains and dense tropical valleys is home to about 14,000 people. The island has seen its fair share of tourism and development. A medical school also draws several hundred students from the U.S. each year. Like elsewhere in the Leewards, fishing is excellent. Blue Marlin, tuna, wahou and swordfish are just a few of the game creatures that habituate the warm waters where the Atlantic Ocean meets the Caribbean Sea.

The union of Antigua and Barbuda achieved independence from Great Britain on November 1, 1981. It remains a member of the British Commonwealth and accordingly recognizes the Queen of England as head of state. Antigua is fairly well developed in comparison to Barbuda, and the sparsely inhabited dependency on Redonda, a tiny island 30 miles east of Antigua. The capital city, St. John's, is a minor international banking center and a favorite British vacation ground.

First inhabited by the Ciboney (Stone people), whose settlements date back to 2400 B.C., Antigua was settled by peaceful Arawaks between the years 50 and 1100. Like elsewhere, the peoples were enslaved and ultimately drove into extinction by a combination of cruelty, neglect, disease and even mass suicide. The fierce Carib Indians apparently never sailed to Antigua or Barbuda.

First sighted by Columbus in 1493, he named the main island Santa Maria de Antigua. Both Spanish and French missionaries attempted to settle it, but were discouraged by the lack of freshwater springs. The first successful towns and farms were established by the British West Indies Company in 1632. After a brief period of French control, the two islands reverted to the British and remained colonies until full independence was achieved.

Sir Christopher Codrington established the first large sugar estate in Antigua in 1674, and leased Barbuda "for one fat sheep per year". He and others brought slaves from Africa to work Antigua's plantations. To exploit the land for sugarcane production, plantation owners cleared the forest and woods. Today, many Antiguans blame frequent droughts on the island's lack of trees to attract rainfall.

Antiguan slaves were emancipated in 1834 but remained bound to their plantation owners. Economic op-

St. Kitts-Nevis

portunities for the new free men were limited by a lack of surplus farming land, no access to credit and an economy built on agriculture rather than manufacturing. Poor labor conditions persisted until 1939, when a member of the royal commission urged the formation of a trade union movement. The Antigua Trades and Labor Union formed shortly afterward and became the political vehicle for Vere Cornwall Bird, the union's president in 1943. The Antigua Labour Party (ALP) first ran candidates in the 1946 elections, beginning a long history of electoral victories. Though he was voted out of office in the 1971 general elections that swept the Progressive Labor Movement into power, Bird and the ALP returned to office in 1976 and again in 1984.

Both islands are home to a myriad of bird species, from tropical mocking birds to oyster catchers. Ten varieties of duck and numerous nesting spots attract ornithologists from around the world. Today Antigua is a colorful island with much to offer. Its famous English Harbor and Admiral Nelson's dockyards are an ideal boaters paradise. Old Fort James, which stood the test of many battles still looks out over St. John's rugged shoreline. Barbuda is smaller and quieter than her sister, and much less hilly. Its distance from Antigua (75 miles) assures it a measure of autonomy. Its main town of Codrington retains a colonial flavor, even if there are only about 2,000 residents to enjoy it.

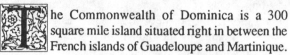

The Commonwealth of Dominica is a 300 square mile island situated right in between the French islands of Guadeloupe and Martinique. Columbus named the island in 1493 after the Sabbath day. Its forbidding interior of rugged hills and dense forests has limited development principally to the coastal plains of its eastern and western shores. The island is famous for its banana and lime exports and quiet white sand beaches. It is also known for the illicit cultivation of marijuana.

After almost 200 years of French, Spanish, and Dutch control, Dominica became a British Colony in 1805. Its central position in the Lesser Antilles archipelago made it a favorite British naval base for attacking pirate ships. The main town of Roseau was first established by France as a weigh station for produce and lumber. Over the years, smaller fishing and lumber mill camps were estab-

lished around the entire perimeter of the island. Despite its geographic location, it remained largely isolated.

Dominica is the largest and northernmost of the Windward Islands, but it is still only 29 miles long and 15 miles wide. Its surface is dominated by a series of high volcanic peaks over which grow rich forests and a variety of flora. The island is a favorite for river rafting, mountain climbing and bird watching.

Dominica gained self-government in 1967. A five-year period of transition led to complete independence from Great Britain in 1978. Political discontent from lack of development shook the first elected government of Patrick R. John, the country's first prime minister. The problems were further compounded by the severe impact of Hurricane David in 1979 and Allen in 1980. That same year, the Dominican Freedom Party under Mary Eugenia Charles came to power. Prime Minister Charles became the first female leader in the West Indies and since she is also the foreign minister and economics and development minister, she was certainly the most accomplished.

In 1981, a bizarre coup attempt was uncovered by U.S. and Dominican authorities. As if the past were repeating itself, a motley crew of neo-nazis, black terrorists and drug king-pins planned to seize the island and convert it into an illegal offshore empire. Among those indicted for conspiracy in the takeover was ex-Prime Minister John himself. U.S. aid and the benefits of President Reagan's Caribbean Basin Initiative have allowed Dominica a period of stability and prosperity never experienced before. In 1984, Prime Minister Charles' conservative party was re-elected to govern this island of 80,000 inhabitants.

Today, St. Lucia and St. Vincent and the Grenadines are each independent nation within the Great Britain's Commonwealth of Nations The story of their development, as one might expect, closely mirrors that of Dominica. The most interesting fact about St. Lucia is that it was not discovered and named by Christopher Columbus. Rather, it was founded in 1502 by another Spanish sea captain named Juan de la Cosa, who explored the Windwards south to the South American mainland.

The Dutch, English and French all tried to establish trading outposts on St. Lucia in the 17th century but faced opposition from hostile Caribs. Small English groups were massacred by the Indians in 1605 and 1640. The French, who had claimed the island, established a successful settlement in 1651 as an offshoot of the colony in neighboring Martinique. For the next century and a half, ownership was hotly disputed between France and England, with the Caribs receding gradually into obscurity and eventual extinction. The island changed hands 14 times up to 1814, when the British finally gained supremacy in the Treaty of Paris. France, which had controlled the island during most of those years, left a strong hint of French culture still apparent in the Roman Catholic Church, the system of law and the Creole patois spoken by the majority.

The British, with their headquarters in Barbados, and the French, centered on Martinique, found St. Lucia even more attractive when the sugar industry developed in

1765. Declared neutral by the Treaty of Paris in 1763, the island was annexed to Martinique in 1765. By 1780, almost 50 sugarcane estates were established on the island, and although most were severely damaged in a devastating hurricane that year, they were quickly re-established. Heavy labor needs of the estates led to large scale importation of blacks from West Africa, a trade that ended in the early 19th century as a prelude to complete emancipation in 1838.

British influence gradually spread once St. Lucia was under its control. English commercial law was introduced in 1827, criminal procedures in 1833, and in 1838, the French language was officially abolished. In that year, St. Lucia was incorporated into the British Windward Islands Administration, with its headquarters in Barbados. The system lasted until 1884, when the Windwards capital was moved to Grenada.

The coal industry proved an economic boon to St. Lucia in the late 19th century. As a convenient location for coal bunkering, Castries Harbor was the major such port in the West Indies until the industry declined with the opening of the Panama Canal and died with the increased use of oil and diesel fuels. Indentured labor from India and China were thus forced to fend for themselves, as were the freed slaves. Over time they each founded new settlements and quietly subsisted the best they could.

St. Lucia's early 20th century history was marked by increasing self-government. A 1924 constitution gave the island its first form of representative government, with a minority of elected members provided for the previously all-nominated Legislative Council. That system, although modified, continued until 1951 when universal adult suffrage was introduced and elected members became a majority in the body. Ministerial government was introduced in 1956, and in 1958, St. Lucia joined the short-lived West Indies Federation, a semi-autonomous dependency of the United Kingdom. When that collapsed in 1962 following Jamaica's refusal to join, a smaller federation was briefly attempted. After the second failure, the United Kingdom and the six Windward and Leeward Islands -- Grenada, St. Vincent, Dominica, Antigua, St. Kitts-Nevis-Anguilla and St. Lucia--developed a novel form of cooperation called "associated statehood".

As an associated state of the United Kingdom from 1967 to 1979, St. Lucia had full responsibility for internal self-government, but left its external affairs and defense responsibilities to Great Britain. Independence was gained in 1979, but St. Lucia remains a member of the Commonwealth. The island's 238 square miles are an array of rugged, volcanic mountains and broad fertile valleys. Like elsewhere on the Windwards, English is the official language, but a significant majority still speak an English/French patois mixture.

St. Vincent and the many small isles sprawling beneath it, called the Grenadines, also achieved independence in 1979. Like St. Lucia, they chose to remain a member of the British Commonwealth. Though politically distinct from St. Lucia, St. Vincent shares an almost identical historical pattern. The capital city of Kingstown retains its 19th century style and has a magnificent botanical garden full of specimens from all over the West Indies. For some odd reason, St. Vincent became the first island to grow breadfruit imported from Polynesia. Breadfruit quickly competed with cavasa as the major wheat substitute in the West Indies until flour imports were commenced in the 1920's. Kingstown is also known for its fine old church buildings and the massive Fort Charlotte overlooking the capital from a height of 600 feet. The west coast fishing village of Layou is the site of several large stone ruins, which are believed to have been sacrificial altars of the Caribs.

The Grenadines consist of almost 100 islets, some of them hardly specks on the map. The chief isles north to south are Bequia, Mustique, Canovan, Mayreau, Union Island and Carrialou. Most of the other isles are privately owned and may not be visited except by written permission. In the early years, the Grenadines supported small whaling crews and oil stations. From time to time, pirates used them as hideouts. There is little development on the islands, except some new condominium projects and boating marinas. The difficulty of producing agriculture on these isles has made fishing the principal livelihood of their 6,000 scattered inhabitants.

Grenada is the smallest independent country in the Western Hemisphere. It is perhaps more widely known because of the U.S. invasion in October, 1983 which followed two weeks of severe political instability. Grenada is actually the largest and southernmost of the Grenadines Islands, but it was always administered separately by the British. The island is traversed by a mountain range that forms a spine down its entire length. The central region is a verdant rainforest.

Columbus discovered Grenada in 1498 during his third voyage to the New World. He named the island Concepcion. The origin of the island's name is obscure. Legend has it that the Spanish renamed the island for the city of Granada, but by the beginning of the 18th century, the name had changed in common usage to Grenada. At the time of discovery, Grenada was inhabited by Caribs, who had driven the more peaceful Arawaks from the island. Partly because of the Caribs, Grenada remained uncolonized for more than 100 years after its discovery. The British attempted to settle the island but were driven away. In 1650, a French company founded by Cardinal Richelieu purchased Grenada from the British and established a small settlement. After several skirmishes with the Caribs, the French brought reinforcements from Martinique and slaughtered the entire Indian population. The island remained under French control until captured by the British a century later during the Seven Year War. Grenada was formally ceded to Great Britain in 1763 by the Treaty of Paris. Although the French regained control in 1779, the island was restored to Great Britain in 1783 by the Treaty of Versailles.

During the 18th century, Grenada's economy underwent an important transition. Like the rest of the West Indies, it was originally settled to cultivate sugar. However, a series of natural disasters paved the way for the introduction of other crops. A plague of ants and a long drought followed by a hurricane, virtually destroyed the sugar industry.

In 1782, Sir Joseph Banks, the botanical adviser to King George III, introduced nutmeg to Grenada. The island's soil proved ideal for growing the spice and because Grenada was a closer source of spices for Europe than the Dutch East Indies, the island assumed a new importance to European traders. The collapse of the sugar estates and the introduction of nutmeg and cocoa encouraged the development of smaller land tenancies. As farmers became land owners, the island developed a relative middle class that became the basis of contemporary Grenadian society.

In 1833, Grenada was made part of the Windward Islands Administration. The governor of the Windward Islands administered the island throughout the remainder of the colonial period. In 1958, the Windward Islands Administration was dissolved, and Grenada joined the Federation of the West Indies. After the federation collapsed in 1962, the British attempted to form a small federation among their remaining dependencies in the eastern Caribbean. Following the failure of this second effort, Grenada became an associated state of Britain in 1967. Under the Associated Statehood Act of 1967, Grenada was granted full autonomy over its internal affairs. It was the first of the associated states to seek full

View of Roseau, capital city of Dominica, 1837.

independence, which Britain granted on February 7, 1974.

The elected government of Sir Eric Gairy was overthrown in a bloodless *coup d'etat* on March 13, 1979. Under the lead of Maurice Bishop, the Marxist New Jewel (Joint Endeavor for Welfare, Education and Liberation) established one party rule and close ties to Cuba. In October 1983, an internal power struggle resulted in the execution of Prime Minister Bishop and several cabinet officers. The resulting instability prompted the U.S. Marines, in cooperation with forces from the Organization of Eastern Caribbean States, to land on Grenada and quickly take control of the island. After a brief occupation and with the support of the overwhelming majority of the Grenadines, the former British Governor General was invited to form an interim government until elections were held in December 1984. Today, spurred by U.S. economic assistance, Grenada is making slow progress in the effort to overcome centuries of developmental neglect.

Grenada and the southern Grenadines

FRENCH ANTILLES

MARIGOT
ST. MARTIN

ST. BARTHELEMY
(ST. BARTS)
Gustavia

GUADELOUPE

Port-Louis

ATLANTIC OCEAN

Ste.-Rose

Deshayes

GRAND-TERRE

LA DESIRADE

St.-Francois

Ste.-Anne

ILES DE
LA PETITE TERRE

BASSE-TERRE

Basse-Terre

N

MARIE GALANTE

CARIBBEAN SEA

ILES DES SAINTES

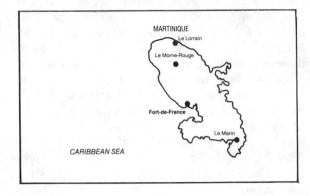

MARTINIQUE

Le Lorrain

Le Morne-Rouge

Fort-de-France

Le Marin

CARIBBEAN SEA

The two French possessions in the Caribbean Sea are Guadeloupe (which is in the Leeward Chain) and Martinique (in the Windward Chain). Guadeloupe is actually two islands, or more accurately, two lobes which in time grew together. The volcanic western half is called Basse-Terre; the flat limestone eastern half is called Grande-Terre. The two are separated by a narrow saltwater stream named the Riviere Salee. A number of smaller isles are attached to Guadeloupe as dependencies. They are Marie-Galante, the Saints Isles, Petite Terre, Desirade, St. Barthelemy and the northern half of St. Martin.* French Guiana is

*The southern half of St.Martin is still a Dutch colony. Its name, therefore, maintains the different spelling of St. Maarten. With no barriers or custom inspectors between them, the differences rest principally in terms of political influence.

the only European colony remaining on the two great continents of the Western Hemisphere. It lays just north of the equator between Suriname (formerly Dutch Guiana) and Brazil on the northeast edge of South America. Like her two sisters, Suriname and Guyana, French Guiana is a wild and mountainous land which remains largely unsettled. The dense tropical rainforests of their interiors make it unlikely that development will extend beyond coastal plains and river basin regions. French Guiana is perhaps best known as the launch site for European space exploration efforts. The capital city and chief port is Cayenne (pronounced Kai-An).

The Arawaks were among the dominant Indian nations in French Guiana, they migrated to Martinique about the beginning of the Christian era. A peaceful people known for their pottery and other crafts, the Arawaks lived tranquilly in the French Antilles for about

1,000 years. They were supplanted by the warlike Carib Indians, whose migrations took them from the Amazon to the northeast shoulder of South America and thence to the Antilles, where they were still arriving during the voyages of Christopher Columbus. Only a handful of Arawak descendants are still living in French Guiana today. After stiff resistance, the Caribs fled or were killed by the first European settlers of the Antilles in the 17th century. No Indian settlements remain in the French Antilles, and the Amerindian population in French Guiana consists of about 3,000, belonging to six tribes. The term "Amerindians" is used to distinguish them from the East Indians who came to work the plantations after the abolition of slavery. Columbus sighted Guadeloupe in 1493, Martinique in 1493 or 1502, and the Guiana coast probably during his third voyage in 1498. The area was permanently settled by the French in the mid-17th century.

The name Martinique derives from an old Carib word meaning "island of flowers." Except for three short periods of British occupation, Martinique has been a French possession since 1635, when mariner Belain D'Esnambuc took the island for France.

The American colonies had close relations with Martinique and the French Antilles. With the advent of the Revolutionary War, the Continental Congress commissioned William Bingham of New York in 1776 to represent the fledgling American government in Martinique. In 1781, a French fleet sailed from Martinique to blockade the British forces at Yorktown, thereby ensuring the victory of General Washington. Overlooking the Fort de France Bay was the plantation of the Tashcer de la Pageria family, whose daughter Josephine was to become the first wife of Napoleon I and Empress of France.

In 1902, Mt. Pelee erupted in the north of the island and in a matter of minutes killed 30,000 people and destroyed Saint-Pierre, the "pearl of the Antilles," then the largest town and commercial and cultural capital of Martinique. President Theodore Roosevelt obtained an emergency grant from the U.S. Congress and two U.S. Navy ships set sail immediately to provide relief, but there were few survivors. Today, Saint-Pierre is a quiet tourist center with fewer than 7,000 residents.

Guadeloupe was known to its Indian inhabitants as Karukera, or "isle of good waters." Columbus named it after the saint whose day it was when he landed, Santa Maria de Guadeloupe de Emstremadura. In 1635, Jean de Plessis and Charles Lienard took possession of the island in the name of the Compagnie des Iles d'Amerique. The first slaves were brought from Africa to work the plantations around 1650 and the first slave rebellion occurred in 1656. Guadeloupe was poorly administered in its early days and was a dependency of Martinique until 1775. In 1794, following a slave revolt and a short period of British occupation, Victor Hughes (nicknamed "The Terrible") arrived from the revolutionary government in Paris complete with portable guillotine, which he used on a number of white planters, and proclaimed the abolition of slavery. In 1802, Napoleon re-established slavery. In 1848, it was finally abolished in all French possessions, due in large measure to the work of abolitionist National Assembly deputy from Guadeloupe and Martinique, Victor Schoelcher, whose memory is commemorated by monuments, street names, and public parks in all corners of the French Antilles. Guadeloupe again settled into a plantation economy following the Napoleonic wars, but unlike in Martinique, where the white planting class had been preserved in part by the British occupation, a significant portion was owned by large firms or absentee landlords, because planters from Guadeloupe had been decimated by or had fled from the revolutionary terror.

France's first settlement of French Guiana was attempted in 1604, but the settlers fled the inhospitable climate and native population the following year. The first permanent settlement began in 1634 and in 1664 the town of Cayenne was established. Agricultural Jesuit settlements flourished in the succeeding years until the Order was expelled from France in 1767. A badly planned and organized settlement in the region of Kourou perished in 1763. Following the abolition of slavery in 1848, the fragile plantation economy declined precipitously. The penal colony known in English as "Devil's Island" was established at Kourou in 1852 and some

70,000 prisoners were shipped to French Guiana before the colony's abolition in 1947. In 1964, Kourou was chosen as the site of the French (and later Euro-French) space center, which brought a substantial increase in population and relative prosperity to the immediate area. In 1977, the first of two settlements of Hmong refugees from Indochina was established in the hilly forests at Cacao, southwest of Cayenne. A third Hmong settlement was started near coastal Mana in the northern tip of the department in 1979.

French Guiana, Guadeloupe, and Martinique are classified as overseas departments of France and since 1946 have been integral parts of the French Republic. St. Martin is a sub-department of Guadeloupe. It was said to be discovered by Columbus on St. Martin's Day in 1493 and subsequently named San Martino. Spain evacuated the island in the 1620's in favor of Puerto Rico's comparative wealth. The Dutch and French laid claim to it thereafter and remain firmly in place to this day. St. Martin/St. Maarten is the smallest territory in the world to be shared by two sovereign nations. In 1972, the metropolitan departments of France were combined in 22 regions with an elected regional council for each. The three French overseas departments in the Caribbean, however, could not agree upon a single regional council to represent them, with the result that each became a region as well as a department. In 1982, the French National Assembly passed a law providing that the overseas regions would elect representatives in proportion to the number of region-wide votes received by each party. The new regional councils have 41 members each in Guadeloupe and Martinique and 34 in French Guiana. Guadeloupe and Martinique each elect two senators to the French Senate and three deputies to the National Assembly. French Guiana elects one senator and one deputy.

The senior central government official in each overseas department is the Commissioner of the Republic, a new title created for all departments of France in 1982 to replace that of "prefect," as part of the new decentralization policy. The commissioner is appointed from Paris for an indefinite period, usually for two to three years, and is normally a career civil servant. Many administrative powers previously held by the prefect are in the process of being delegated to the regional and general councils.

Though sugar cane, bananas, light industry and tourism have all been developed in the French Antilles, they are not self sufficient. Like other islands, the population of Martinique and Guadeloupe is a mixture of African, French, Indian, Chinese and others. French and Creole Patois are their two main languages. Their hospitable nature and friendly smiles make the islands popular tourist sites.

St Ann's Fort built by the British in the early eighteenth century.

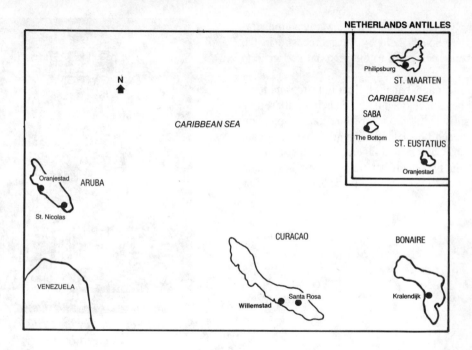

NETHERLANDS ANTILLES

N

ST. MAARTEN
Philipsburg

CARIBBEAN SEA

SABA
The Bottom

ST. EUSTATIUS
Oranjestad

CARIBBEAN SEA

ARUBA
Oranjestad
St. Nicolas

VENEZUELA

CURACAO
Willemstad Santa Rosa

BONAIRE
Kralendijk

Page 72

he Netherlands Antilles are two distinct groups of five islands and part of a sixth which are separated by about 500 miles of sea. The southern three - Aruba, Bonaire and Curacao - are just north of Venezuela territorial waters. They are sometimes called the "ABC islands" for short. The northern possessions known as the "Three S's," are actually part of the Leeward chain, but the Dutch call them the Windwards. As mentioned earlier, the sovereignty on the island of St. Maarten is divided between France and the Netherlands. The islands, along with Dutch Guiana were adiministered by the government in Amsterdam until 1954. After that time, Dutch Guiana and a federation of the islands were made equal partners in the Dutch Kingdom. Colonial rule was quickly abolished and local autonomy commenced. Independence referenda in the 1980's failed to pass on any of the islands. In 1986, however, Aruba obtained self-rule and voted to become fully independent in ten years.

The racially mixed population of the islands contains people of European, African, Amerindian and East Asian stock. Obviously, both groups of islands inherited a great many characteristics from their neighbors. Thus, latin influence is strongest on the ABC islands while Afro-British influence is greater in the northern group. Curacao is the most populous isle with a population of about 175,000. Willemstad, the capital city, is located on the southeastern coast. Aruba, with 6,500 people ,is second in terms of population but is more widely known. Its capital city is Orenjestad, which is served by daily flights to Amsterdam. Aruba has a reputation for being a genuine international resort island. Visitors come from North and South America, Europe and Australia to enjoy the tropical splendor. The only complaint heard is that it is not cheap. The third island, Bonaire is the most arid and the smallest of the group. Its capital city is named after a Dutch captain Kralendjik. The official language is Dutch, but a large percentage of the ABC islands speak "Papiamento," an unusual mixture of Dutch, Spanish, Portuguese and English. The economies of the islands are driven almost exclusively by the processing and transport of Venezuelan petroleum.

Prior to the arrival of the Dutch and the Spaniards before them, the ABC islands were inhabited by a breed of Arawaks called the Caquetio, who immigrated from Venezuela. These people were forcibly evacuated by the Spaniards to Santo Domingo in 1513 to work as slaves in copper mines. In 1635, the Dutch took possession of Curacao after losing a sea battle with Spain in the Windwards. As a defensive measure, the Dutch also occupied Bonaire and Aruba the following year.

Soon Curacao became the Netherlands major slave trading market and auction center. It is estimated that between 1675 and 1715, more than 80,000 captured Africans were "processed" through Curacao. The Dutch West Indies Company also prospered in commodities such as salt, arrowroot, corn, bananas and livestock. In conjunction with her embattled territories in the North, such as St. Eustatius and Saba, the Dutch traded with American settlers in violation of Spanish and British law. As always, the convulsion of the 15th and 16th centuries caused many sea battles in which possession of the Dutch Antilles changed hands. So small was the male population of the three S's that they were nicknamed the Isles of the Women. However, the Dutch proved able defenders and by 1815 all her possessions were regained.*

Each island slowly achieved its own identity and purpose. Curacao, for example, became a commercial port. Aruba was used for agriculture and Bonaire primarily for fishing and salt panning. With the abolishment of slavery by 1863, all three islands became more dependent on government aid from The Hague. Shipping de-

*St. Eustatius for example, a speck of an island at the top of the Leeward arc, changed hands twenty times by 1800.

clined markedly and trade became more localized as a result. Then in the early 1900's oil was discovered beneath the coastal waters of Venezuela. In 1915, Shell Oil Company opened the first refinery on Curacao. Standard Oil followed by building another on Aruba. Suddenly, the islands were of great economic importance. A comparative measure of prosperity followed, with local development and diversification out pacing all its Caribbean cousins.

After World War II, tourism arrived in Aruba and elsewhere. The rise of the cruise ships brought substantial air traffic to the islands as an embarkation point. Bonaire followed suit and by the 1960's had more tourists than flamingos. Willemstad is still considered the most "European" city in the Caribbean.

Dutch Guiana became the independent state of Suriname in 1975. Though it is the smallest state in South America, it immediately became its most democratic. Then suddenly in 1980, a leftist military group ousted the elected government in a violent coup de' etat. Most western capital was nationalized and relations between

Aruba woman preparing bananas for export.

Surinam and the U.S. became strained. However, elections in 1986 and a commitment by the government to return to constitutional rule helped alleviate a large margin of regional distrust. interestingly, the Netherlands first acquired the territory of Suriname from Great Britain in a swap for New Netherlands (New York) on the North American mainland in 1677.

An island confederation was established in 1954 and resulted in an all-island legislature on Curacao called the "Staten," while each maintained its own island council for local rule. The confederation also was granted permanent representation in the Dutch Parliament. Like the British model, the Netherlands maintains responsibility for defense and international affairs.

The "Three S's" remain connected to their distant neighbors only by law. Saba and St. Eustatius (called Statia by her inhabitants) are both very small and contain no meadows, pastures or woodlands. They are home to only about 10,000 people. Their most prominent feature is a few large homes for vacationing Dutch aristocrats. St. Maarten is more developed and has a more diversified economy. It remains divided between France (northern half) and the Netherlands because in 1674 neither side had the necessary supplies or strength to drive the other off. The present boundary, while completely open, was literally stepped-off by a soldier for each side to settle a territorial dispute. Despite the numerous battles that engulfed the region for 300 years, it remained remarkably peaceful. Philipsburg, its capital city, is home to almost 25,000 people. Its airport is now the second busiest in the Caribbean. Tourism and service industries account for most of the employment, though the three islands are still heavily reliant on Dutch financial support.

The twin island nation of Trinidad and Tobago has grown to become one of the most interesting and popular destinations in the Caribbean. Lying only seven miles off the coat of Venezuela, Trinidad is lush and tropical. Its capital, Port-of-Spain is the second largest city in the Caribbean in terms of population and commercial trade. Only San Juan, Puerto Rico is bigger. But what it lacks in figures, Port-of-Spain makes up in sheer variety. Visitors to the capital are surprised to find Moslem mosques, Hindu temples and gingerbread-style Victorian mansions.

Tobago rests 21 miles to the northeast, a mere one-sixteenth the size of Trinidad, its gently sloping hills and sleepy towns are substantially more remote and quiet. A mile off Tobago's northwest coast is Buccoo Reef, which forms a magnificent natural breakwater and wildlife preserve. Little Tobago, a tiny island off its shore is the only place other than New Guinea where the beautiful Bird of Paradise maintains a natural habitat. Each year, the Carnival Festival in March brings out the nation's citizens for traditional dance and music. The Limbo and Calypso music, now enjoyed worldwide, owe their origin to the people of Trinidad and Tobago. It's been said that no people know how to celebrate better than they.

Columbus discovered Trinidad in 1498 on his third voyage to the New World and took possession of it on behalf of Spain. At the time it was inhabited by the warlike Caribs, who are said to have christened the island *Lere* (Land of the Humming Bird). Columbus called the island La Trinidad in honor of the Holy Trinity because his first sight of it was the three mountain peaks on its southern mountain range.

When it became clear that there was no mineral wealth in Trinidad, the Spaniards neglected their discovery for nearly a hundred years until, in 1584, the first permanent settlement was established on the banks of the Caroni

River and named San Jose de Oruna (now St. Joseph). The Spaniards enslaved the natives to work their tobacco and cocoa plantations, but repeated crop failures and a rapid decline in the Indian population kept the island in a state of poverty.

In 1783, the Spanish Crown issued a royal proclamation permitting colonization by Roman Catholics. Generous land grants were offered to those who promised to develop the island's agricultural and commercial potential. The importation of slave labor was officially encouraged. Planters and their slaves from Haiti and other French possessions came by the thousands to settle in Trinidad and brought with them their knowledge of sugar cane cultivation. Soon the island began to prosper and the capital was moved to its present site. By 1834, when slavery was abolished, the slave population of Trinidad and Tobago combined had grown to 26,000.

In 1797, after the Napoleonic wars began, a British expedition came to Trinidad and easily captured the island. Trinidad's first contact with the British had been in 1595 when Sir Walter Raleigh, in search of the fabled

El Dorado, patched his ships at Pitch Lake--even today a major supplier of asphalt for the world market--and went on to loot and burn St. Joseph. The territory was ceded to Great Britain by Spain in 1802 and was to remain under British control for the next 160 years. The Afro-Hispano-Gallic way of life continued to flourish, for it was many years before the British altered the official language and laws.

The end of slavery had a profound impact on the islands. Freed men found it difficult to accept the minimal offers of the estate owners. Thus, most ex-slaves found themselves in a sorry state, not unlike their kind throughout the region. It was the resulting shortage in the labor supply that began the transformation of Trinidad into the miniature United Nations it is today. Between 1845 and 1917, the British Government subsidized the immigration of some 145,000 East Indians to Trinidad under the indenture system. They had been thought to be the ethnic group most apt to withstand the harsh demands of "King Sugar," and many stayed on after their period of indenture, when land was offered

The unique sound of steel drums can be heard everywhere in Trinidad.

them in lieu of passage home. Early attempts to introduce a labor supply from China and Portugal were largely unsuccessful; most of those immigrants ended up in commercial activities. More recently a fairly large number of Middle Eastern immigrants have settled in Trinidad. Although they represent nearly every Eastern Mediterranean nationality, the majority of them have come from Syria and Lebanon.

Tobago's history was not linked to Trinidad's until 1889, when it was administratively united with the larger island. It is said that Columbus sighted Tobago in 1498 without landing on it, but the credit for its discovery belongs to an Englishman, Captain John Keymis. During the 17th century it passed successively through the hands of Britain, France, Holland and Courland (a former principality of Latvia). The international rivalry stemmed from its strategic importance as a naval fort. Finally, in 1704, deserted and destroyed, it was declared a no-man's land. For a while Tobago was a base for pirates raiding in the South Caribbean and the Spanish Main, but in 1762 the British took possession of the island, ending the most turbulent period in its history.

Plantations were sold or granted to prospective farmers who imported African slaves and began the cultivation of sugar, cotton and indigo. By 1790 some 14,000 of the island's 15,000 inhabitants were West African slaves. Harsh treatment led to several slave insurrections throughout the period. Many folk heroes, poetry and stories of life on the island trace their origin to this struggle.

France captured Tobago again in 1781, retaining possession until the British again took over in 1793. Except for France's brief return in 1802-03, the island remained under British control. The passage of slavery to freedom in Tobago occurred without event and indeed, by 1880 most of the freed Negroes had managed to secure their own plots of land, beginning the first diversification of agriculture. In 1884 the bottom fell out of the sugar industry and most of the planters liquidated or simply left their holdings to the former slaves. Unable to provide for Tobago's administration, the British Government made the small island a ward of Trinidad in 1889. The sugar industry was never revived. The islanders learned to cultivate cocoa and coconuts, the two major export crops today.

Under British rule the two islands received law and order and stable government and underwent the gradual political evolution from Crown Colony to internal self-government in 1962. Trinidad's first decade of liberation began with noticeable enthusiasm, led by Prime Minister Eric E. Williams of the People's National Movement. But the nation's fortunes gradually declined culminating in a short-lived army revolt in 1970. Finally in 1976 ,the country negotiated complete independence from Great Britain. Since that time, Trinidad and Tobago have been at the forefront of economic development and social prosperity in the Caribbean Basin. Boosted by oil and tourist revenue, the 1.25 million citizen of the islands enjoy a higher standard of living than most of their neighbors. Adecine in world-wide petroleum prices in the 1980's took its toll on the economy, pushing the unemployment rose to an unparalleled high of 25 percent. The government of Prime Minister Arthur Robin-son adepted an assterity program and promoted a return to agriculture, which by 1989,employed only about ten precent of the population.

Suddenly, in July 1990, a small group of militant Muslims, angry at what they pereceived as official incompetence, stormed the parliament and seized Robinson, several ministers and about two dozen others. Unable to hold out for the seven day seige, the plotters withdrew their demands and surrender. Within a week the government announced life had return to normal. Despite the upheaval, the country remains one of the most unique and colorful nations in the world.

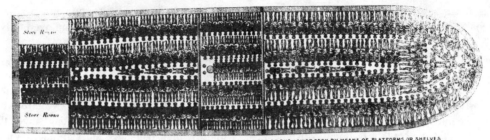

PLAN SHEWING THE STOWAGE OF 130 ADDITIONAL SLAVES ROUND THE WINGS OR SIDES OF THE LOWER DECK BY MEANS OF PLATFORMS OR SHELVES IN THE MANNER OF GALLERIES IN A CHURCH THE SLAVES STOWED ON THE SHELVES AND BELOW THEM HAVE ONLY A HEIGHT OF 2 FEET 7 INCHES BETWEEN THE BEAMS AND FAR LESS UNDER THE BEAMS . *See Fig 1*

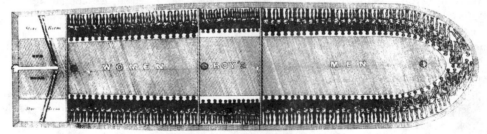

Slaves were packed into ships under inhumane conditions for the "Middle Passage" from Africa to the Americas.

The three territories described in this chapter reflect islands which are geographically and politically unconnected. But because they share the British West Indies heritage, it is convenient to group them together, in this, the last chapter.

Barbados is the most easterly of the West Indies islands and is not typically grouped with any other chain. It is a solitary island of low hills which is actually situated wholly in the Atlantic Ocean. Today, it is one of the most densely populated countries of the world, in relation to its meager 166 square miles.

Its name derives from the Portuguese meaning "bearded ones." It is thought to have been so named due to the beard-like roots of the tropical banyan trees found there. Barbados was first settled by the British in 1627 and 1628 as, deserted island. The Carib Indian inhabitants probably chose to flee rather than fight to retain their homes. Despite a multitude of foreign attacks, it remained under British control for more than 300 years.

After the introduction of sugar cane in 1640, the island prospered and received frequent immigrants from Bermuda, many of whom were Puritans in search of religious freedom. Representative institutions were granted by royal charter under Charles I and the House of Assembly was established in 1639, thus making it the most senior democracy in all the West Indies. Despite the relatively liberal political atmosphere that was created, the island was in reality governed by sugar plantation owners and tradesman. Slaves were imported and Barbados became a major slave auction center during the early heyday of the "middle passage." The principal settlement was Bridgetown in the southwest corner of the island. As the capital city, it has one of the largest metropolitan areas in the region. It was not until the 1930's that a movement for political rights was begun by the descendants of emancipated slaves. One of the leaders of this movement, Sir Grantley Adams, founded the Barbados Labour Party in 1938.

Progress toward more democratic government for Barbados was made in 1951 when universal adult suffrage was introduced. This was followed by steps toward increased self-government culminating in 1961 when Barbados achieved full internal autonomy. From 1958 to 1962, Barbados was one of ten members in the West Indies Federation and Sir Grantley Adams served as the first and only prime minister of the federation. When the federation was terminated, Barbados reverted to its former status as a self-governing colony. Following several attempts to form another federation composed of Barbados and the Leeward and Windward Islands, Barbados negotiated its own independence at a constitutional conference with the United Kingdom in June 1966. After years of peaceful, democratic and evolutionary progress, Barbados attained self rule on November 30, 1966.

The island is blessed with rich soil and tropical beauty.

When the work is done there's time to relax.

Her 275,000 citizens currently enjoy a standard of living higher than any other island in the West Indies. The pear-shaped island has been called "little England", in recognition of the lush, fertile hills and "bobby" style constabulary. Town names like Yorkshire, Windsor, Highgate and of course, Bridgetown, the capital, are quintessentially British. Barbados remains a member of the Commonwealth of Nations.

In the 1750's, George Washington and his sickly elder brother Laurence visited Barbados. The island's pleasant and unvarying climate had been thought at the time to be a health elixir. In his diary, Washington wrote that he was "perfectly enraptured with the beautiful prospects...on every side, the fields of cane, corn and fruit trees in a delightful setting."

The Turks and Caicos Islands are situated in the Atlantic at the southern end of the Bahama sprawl. Geographically, they are comprised of two groups totaling 30 islands, with a combined land area of about 165 square miles. Only eight islands are inhabited. The Turks group is separated on the west from the Caicos by a deep channel twenty two miles across. Like the Bahamas, the islands are low, flat, rocky and inhospitable to planned agriculture. Accordingly, sisal and corn are the two economic mainstays, along with shellfishing and salt-raking made possible by evaporating sea water on the rocks at shore. The islands of Grand Turk, South Caicos and Providenciales (Provo for short) have developed small commercial harbors around which towns have slowly grown. The capital of Cockburn town is the only settlement on Grand Turk island, yet it too remains largely isolated.

The islands were first discovered by Ponce de Leon in 1512. However, no settlement was attempted until 1678 when a group of Bermudians arrived to develop the salt trade. These early settlers were ousted by the French in a series of attacks that culminated in victory in 1764. The islands were then abandoned and reclaimed by British loyalists in flight from the 13 rebellious colonies of America. By the time slavery was abolished in 1834, most white settlers fled once again, this time to other islands or back home to England.

In 1874, the Turks and Caicos Islands were joined to Jamaica for colonial and administrative purposes. When Jamaica obtained independence in 1962, they were made a new colony. In more recent years, a large minority have indicated a preference for independence. They have been met by protestations at home and abroad that the islands are just too poor and too remote to survive on their own. The total population of the islands is only about 10,000.

The Cayman Islands are located in the central Caribbean situated between Jamaica and Cuba. Until 1959, they had been administered from Kingston as Jamaican dependencies. The three islands are Grand Cayman, Cayman Brac and Little Cayman. They were first sighted by Columbus in 1503. Though he did not anchor there, he named the three islands Las Tortegas, because the area was covered with large turtles. They were renamed by the British many years later because Caymans, small alligator-like reptiles, had largely supplanted the turtles as the dominant creatures on the island. No evidence of continued Arawak or other native presence has been found on the Caymans.

The Treaty of Madrid in 1670 ceded the islands to the British Crown. Due to their isolation and lack of prospects, no serious settlement activity occurred until the 19th century. Prior to that time, the islands were a place of last refuge for shipwrecked sailors, marooned buccaneers, exiled debtors and hardluck beachcombers. The capital city, Georgetown is on Grand Cayman which is only 22 miles long and eight miles wide. It was very difficult for the settlers to attract ships and was not uncommon for the harbor to be devoid of visiting ships for years at a time. It is home to 75 percent of Cayman's 25,000 citizens.

The Caymans did not join the pulse of the world until air transport was established there in 1940. The only previous mode of transportation had been steamship from Jamaica. In 1971, the islands were granted marginal self-rule, though they remain a dependency of Great Britain. Since that time, lack of taxes and banking secrecy laws have resulted in a large influx of foreign investment companies and off-shore corporations who maintain ostensible headquarters in Georgetown. Luxury condominiums and beachhouses play host to winter residents from England and the United States. Boating and deep-sea diving are particularly popular tourist attractions as are the magnificent coral reefs surrounding the two smaller islands. Caymanians enjoy one of the highest standards of living in the region.

A World War I memorial in George Town, capital city of the Cayman Islands. Photograph courtesy of Warren Yeager.

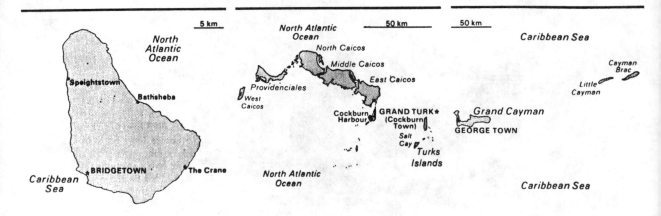

Barbados

5 km

North Atlantic Ocean

Speightstown

Bathsheba

Caribbean Sea

BRIDGETOWN

The Crane

Turks and Caicos Islands

50 km

North Atlantic Ocean

North Caicos

Middle Caicos

East Caicos

Providenciales

West Caicos

Cockburn Harbour

GRAND TURK (Cockburn Town)

Salt Cay

Turks Islands

North Atlantic Ocean

Cayman Islands

50 km

Caribbean Sea

Cayman Brac

Little Cayman

Grand Cayman

GEORGE TOWN

Caribbean Sea

This representation is not geographically accurate.

FURTHER READING

Burns, Sir Alan	History of the British West Indies, Allen & Unwin Ltd., 1965.
Lewis, Gordon K.	The Growth of the Modern West Indies, Modern Reader Paperbacks, 1968.
Lewis, Gordon K.	Mainstreams of Caribbean Thought, John Hopkins U. Press, 1985.
Mitchell, Carleton	Isles of the Caribbees, National Geographic Society, 1971
Parry, J. H. et al.	A Short History of the West Indies, 4th Edition, Macmillan Caribbean, 1987.
Pearey, G. Etzel	The West Indian Scene, D. Van Nostrand Co., 1965.
Poole, Bernard F.	The Caribbean Commission, University of South Carolina Press, 1951.
Rodman, Selden	The Caribbean, Hawthorn Books, 1968.
Waugh, Alec	A Family of Islands, Doubleday, 1964.

This is a short list of other sources. There are countless other interesting older works still available recounting the colonial period first hand. In addition, numerous travel guide books are regularly published and updated which contain information helpful to tourists. The author strongly encourages their use.

ORDER FORM

QUANITY	TITLE	UNIT COST	TOTAL
	Hawaii : A Colorful and Concise History	$3.95	
	The Bahamas : A Colorful and Concise History	3.95	
	The Island of the Caribbean : A Colorful and Concise History	3.95	
	Mexico : A Colorful and Concise History	3.95	

Yes, please send me the books indicated above, Add $1.25 shipping and handling for the first book and $.50 for each additional book. Add $2.00 to total for books shipped to Canada or Hawaii. Overseas postage will be billed. Allow up to 4 weeks for delivery. Send check or money order payable to Scrivener Press. No cash or C.O.D.'s please. Quantity discounts available on request.

Subtotal	
Shipping & Handling	
MI residents add 4% sales tax	
TOTAL	

SEND BOOKS TO

NAME:_____

ADDRESS_____

CITY_____STATE____ZIP_____

Scrivener Press

P.O. Box 37175
Oak Park, MI 48237
(313) 546-9123 FAX (313) 546-3010
Phone orders by credit card : (800) 345-0096

ORDER FORM

QUANITY	TITLE	UNIT COST	TOTAL
	Hawaii : A Colorful and Concise History	$3.95	
	The Bahamas : A Colorful and Concise History	3.95	
	The Island of the Caribbean : A Colorful and Concise History	3.95	
	Mexico : A Colorful and Concise History	3.95	

Yes, please send me the books indicated above, Add $1.25 shipping and handling for the first book and $.50 for each additional book. Add $2.00 to total for books shipped to Canada or Hawaii. Overseas postage will be billed. Allow up to 4 weeks for delivery. Send check or money order payable to Scrivener Press. No cash or C.O.D.'s please. Quantity discounts available on request.

Subtotal	
Shipping & Handling	
MI residents add 4% sales tax	
TOTAL	

SEND BOOKS TO

NAME:_____

ADDRESS_____

CITY_____STATE____ZIP_____

Scrivener Press

P.O. Box 37175
Oak Park, MI 48237
(313) 546-9123 FAX (313) 546-3010
Phone orders by credit card : (800) 345-0096

ORDER FORM

QUANITY	TITLE	UNIT COST	TOTAL
	Hawaii : A Colorful and Concise History	$3.95	
	The Bahamas : A Colorful and Concise History	3.95	
	The Island of the Caribbean : A Colorful and Concise History	3.95	
	Mexico : A Colorful and Concise History	3.95	

Yes, please send me the books indicated above, Add $1.25 shipping and handling for the first book and $.50 for each additional book. Add $2.00 to total for books shipped to Canada or Hawaii. Overseas postage will be billed. Allow up to 4 weeks for delivery. Send check or money order payable to Scrivener Press. No cash or C.O.D.'s please. Quantity discounts available on request.

Subtotal	
Shipping & Handling	
MI residents add 4% sales tax	
TOTAL	

SEND BOOKS TO

NAME:_____

ADDRESS_____

CITY_____STATE_____ZIP_____

Scrivener Press

P.O. Box 37175
Oak Park, MI 48237
(313) 546-9123 FAX (313) 546-3010
Phone orders by credit card : (800) 345-0096